Recipes for Entertaining
PANAMANIAN STYLE

A COLLECTION OF RECIPES
BY SONIA ORTIZ

Recipes for Entertaining Panamanian Style
A Collection of Recipes By Sonia Ortiz

Recipes by Sonia Ortiz
Recipe contributions and photography by James Peshek
Introduction and book design by Enrique de la Espriella
Produced by Enrique de la Espriella

Published by Enrique de la Espriella. Printed in the United States of America.
ISBN 9798986869209 for the hardcover book.
ISBN 9798986869216 for the paperback book.

First Printing: 2022
Updated: January 2024

Recipes for Entertaining
PANAMANIAN STYLE

A Collection of Recipes
by Sonia Ortiz

TABLE OF CONTENTS

Bridge of the America

Panama Canal Miraflores Locks

Santa Maria La Antigua Cathedral

La Garita Beach, Pedasí

INTRODUCTION

By Enrique de la Espriella

Growing up in Panama is a unique gastronomic experience. Known as the "Crossroads of the World" because of the Panama Canal, it has brought to the country rich and unique flavors from all around the globe. I remember eating food from Italy, China, South America, the Caribbean, and of course, the simple but delicious flavors of my own country. I especially fell in love with seafood as it is so plentiful in Panama having both Atlantic and Pacific oceans right in our backyard. This explosion of diverse flavors is perfectly represented in this cookbook. It is important to mention that in no way this book is meant to represent a rule book of Panamanian cuisine, but simply a compilation of my family's beloved recipes.

Starting with an introduction to some of the most important ingredients of the Panamanian kitchen, we quickly follow with the classic Panamanian recipes. Here is where you will find the friduras (fried treats) that I love so much, from Yuca Frita, Hojaldres, and Patacones. All the dishes in this section are by far the most popular in Panama, not forgetting recipes for Tortillas Panameñas and Tamales.

Then the book sets the tone for a gathering of family and friends with some typical and favorite beverages, followed by important sauces and accompaniments that would enhance many of the dishes in this cookbook. Highlights of these include the delicious and nutty flavor of the Achiote Oil used in rice and other recipes to add rich color and unique layers of taste; or the bright green color of the Chimichurri Sauce that goes perfectly with steaks and frituras.

The appetizers, salads, and main dishes include a wide array of options that could be made for everyday meal solutions or extravagant celebrations with a large gathering. One of my childhood favorites is the Parmesan Potato Gratin and the Pasta with Basil Pesto. There is nothing better than grabbing leaves from your own home-grown basil plant and preparing a pesto sauce from scratch. Either one of these recipes would brighten anyone's dreary day. Without question, my favorite in the main dishes section is the Coconut Rice with Raisins, a decadent delight for those looking for a sweeter accompaniment to pork, beef, or fish. But of course, anything seafood in this book is just out of this world, especially the Shrimp Scampi or the Steamed Clams in Garlic Sauce.

For the dessert section, you'll notice the absence of chocolate in the recipes. Locals favor desserts made with fruits and sugars. While I enjoy most recipes in this section, the Merengues and Cocadas Panameñas are by far my favorite because they remind me of my childhood days stopping at Queso Chela on the way to the beach for warm bread and treats for the family.

My family and I come back to these tried and trusted recipes time and time again. I hope you enjoy the recipes of this book as much as our family has had putting them together.

PANAMANIAN STAPLES

With its cosmopolitan lifestyle, country towns of the "interior," warm weather, soft sandy beaches, and the iconic Panama Canal, the country of Panama attracts visitors from around the globe. The resident population is as equally diverse. As a result, the foods commonly found throughout the country represent this varied and dynamic culture. While the traditional cuisine of Panama is very unique and deeply loved, Panamanians are known to embrace a variety of international cuisines from around the world including Spain, China, Japan, India, Italy, and the Americas, among others. Below are some widely used ingredients in both traditional Panamanian cooking as well as other types of cuisines served throughout the nation.

Olives / Aceitunas
Green olives are delicious served on their own, but also lend a briny and salty addition to rice dishes and fillings for empanadas or tamales.

Annatto Seed / Achiote
The brick red colored annatto seed is harvested from the achiote tree and is often used to impart a yellow or orange color to foods along with a distinct flavor. Gently heated in oil to extract their vibrant color, they are then drained with the oil being used for cooking.

Scotch Bonnet or Habanero / Aji Chombo
Ranging in color from yellow to orange to red, the aji chombo adds tons of fiery heat and slight fruitiness. Scotch bonnet or habanero peppers may be used as a substitute.

Avocado / Aguacate
Known for their buttery quality, rich flavor and texture, avocados are a widely prized accompaniment served on their own or as a component of salads and sandwiches. Loaded with fiber, good fats, potassium and other nutrients, the avocado is a deceptively healthy choice.

Capers / Alcaparras
The edible flower bud of a caper tree, capers are usually found either in a brine or salted. Delicious served with fish or chicken, capers also add a burst of vinegary saltiness flavor to pasta sauces, salads, and fillings.

Rice / Arroz
A traditional Panamanian meal would not be complete without some form of rice. Used in side dishes, main courses, or even desserts, rice is an extremely versatile and essential ingredient.

Prunes / Ciruelas Pasas
Known for their intensely sweet flavor, prunes are an excellent complement to stewed meats, adding depth and sweetness.

Culantro

Aji Chombo

Coconut / Coco

From sweet coconut candies to rice made with coconut milk, you will find coconut added to a variety of foods and beverages. Don't miss the chance to sample an icy cold fresh young coconut being sold on roadsides or at the beach served with a straw to sip the refreshing and delicious coconut water.

Long-leaf Cilantro / Culantro

Similar in flavor to cilantro, culantro has a more intense flavor and aroma that lends itself well for use during the cooking process. Culantro has long serrated and prickly leaves that can be chopped and added to a sofrito, a pot of beans, or used in a chimichurri sauce.

Milk Caramel / Dulce de Leche

Prepared by slowly heating sweetened milk, the milk and sugar caramelizes into a thick and sweet spread. Most supermarkets carry a much more convenient and tasty prepared version, usually found near the condensed milk.

Assorted Spices / Especias de Hierbas Variadas

The diverse flavors of the Panamanian kitchen are enhanced by an extensive variety of herbs and spices. Sweet spices of cinnamon, cloves, and star anise are often complemented with savory herbs and spices including coriander, cumin, and bay leaves.

Maria Cookies / Galletas Maria

Maria cookies are round, slightly-sweet cookies, similar in taste to a graham cracker. Maria cookies are pervasive in Latin America, and are used in countless dessert recipes or often eaten as a snack.

Pigeon Peas / Guandú

A legume, almost always cooked with rice, the pigeon pea has a mild flavor and pleasing aroma. The high protein content makes it an excellent addition to a healthy Panamanian diet.

Evaporated Milk / Leche Evaporada

With more than half of the water removed, shelf-stable evaporated milk adds intense creaminess to flans, egg nog, and scalloped potatoes. With or without the addition of water, it can be substituted for milk in most recipes, or also used as a delicious creamer for a morning coffee or tea.

Dried Corn / Maiz Seco

After being soaked, cooked, and ground, corn is the source of many traditional foods including tortillas, empanadas, and tamales.

Mango

Mango trees are found throughout the country and thus the mango is ubiquitous in the Panamanian diet. Perfectly ripe mangoes have a syrupy sweetness with a firm yet tender flesh. An unripe mango can also be made into a quick pickle or used in salads. Frequently sold by the bagful on the roadside, mangoes are an inexpensive and refreshing treat.

Guinea Yam / Ñame

Ñame typically has a rough, dark brown skin with a creamy or yellowish colored flesh, and a texture similar to a potato. Its flavor is mild, somewhat nutty with a slightly chewy texture. Ñame is often used in Panamanian soups and stews.

Taro Root / Otoe

Otoe is a starchy root vegetable, also known as taro root. It is brown skinned with a white or pinkish flesh that, when cooked, is similar to a potato, making it the perfect choice for a soup or stew.

Raisins / Pasas

Typically thought of as an addition to sweets and breads, raisins bring subtly surprising sweetness when added to savory dishes as well.

Ripe Plantain / Platano Maduro

Delicious black skinned plantains have ripened to a subtle sweetness which is accentuated when fried, sautéed, or baked.

Green Plantain / Platano Verde

Not to be mistaken for a green banana, the plantain is starchy and hard, and is not meant to be eaten raw. Cut into chunks, fried, then smashed, making patacones (or tostones as it is often called in other countries) is the most frequent use.

Fresh Farmer's Cheese / Queso Fresco

With its salty and mild, yet slightly tangy flavor, queso fresco can be sliced and served with Panamanian tortillas or crumbled on salads, vegetables, or stews.

Hot Sauce / Salsa Picante

The table would not be complete without a bottle of Panama's own hot sauce, D'Elidas. Often added to stews, soups, and tamales, a few drops of this fiery sauce will liven up any dish.

Yucca / Yuca

A starchy tubular root, which has similar qualities to a potato, but is denser and more fibrous. Yuca can be found fresh with its dark, tough skin still intact, or more conveniently frozen and ready to be cooked in stews, mashed, steamed, or fried.

Spices

PANAMANIAN FAVORITES

STUFFED YUCCA FRITTERS

Carimañolas

1 pound frozen yucca

3 cloves garlic

1 tablespoon salt

2 tablespoons tomato paste

½ medium onion

1 teaspoon salt

½ green bell pepper

½ teaspoon black pepper

2 tablespoons diced pimentos

½ pound lean ground beef

3 tablespoons chopped culantro

2 tablespoons achiote oil or olive oil

Place yucca in a large stock pot, add salt and cover with water. Boil for 30 to 40 minutes, until tender when pierced with the tip of a knife. Drain, reserving 1 cup of cooking liquid. Place warm yucca in a large mixing bowl. Cut any large pieces of yucca in half and remove tough fibrous pieces from the center of the yucca. Mash with a potato masher until smooth. Lightly knead dough until it forms a ball, using cornstarch as needed to prevent sticking. Cover and set aside to cool.

Add onion, green pepper, pimentos, culantro, garlic, tomato paste, salt, and pepper to the bowl of a food processor fixed with a steel blade. Pulse several times until finely chopped and almost smooth.

Heat achiote oil in a large skillet over medium-high heat. Add ground beef, season with salt and pepper, and cook until browned, breaking up any large pieces. Add prepared vegetable mixture and sauté for 4 to 5 minutes until vegetables have softened and any liquid has evaporated from the pan. Set aside to cool completely.

Using lightly oiled hands, form ⅓ cup of dough into 4- to 5-inch discs of yucca dough about ¼-inch thick. Add about two tablespoons of meat mixture to the center of the dough circle. Using your fingers, bring the sides of the dough together and shape the fritter to form a thick cylinder about 3-inches long, ensuring all edges are sealed. Use additional cornstarch as needed to prevent sticking. Repeat with remaining dough and meat.

Heat 1 inch of oil to 350° F in a large skillet over medium heat. Carefully add 3 to 4 fritters to the oil and cook for 4 to 5 minutes on each side until lightly golden brown. Drain on paper towel and keep warm while remaining fritters are fried.

CRISPY FRIED YUCCA
Yuca Frita

2 pounds frozen yucca

1 tablespoon salt

Oil for frying

Place the yucca in a stock pot, cover with water and add salt. Bring to a boil over high heat and cook until tender, about 20 to 30 minutes. Drain well. Cut into 1-inch thick pieces, removing the fibrous center from each piece.

Using a deep fryer or high sided pan, heat oil to 375° F. Fry in batches until golden brown. Drain on a paper towel–lined pan and season with salt.

Serve with Chimichurri or other dipping sauce.

PANAMANIAN FRIED BREAD
Hojaldres

2 cups all-purpose flour

1 teaspoon salt

2 teaspoons baking powder

2 teaspoons granulated sugar

1 tablespoon vegetable oil

¾ cup water

Oil for frying

Add flour, salt, baking powder, and sugar to a large mixing bowl. Whisk to combine. Add oil and ¾ cup of the water. Mix using your hands until the flour is moistened. Pour mixture out onto a board and knead for several minutes until the mixture forms a smooth dough. Return the dough to the mixing bowl, lightly brush the top with oil and cover with a towel or plastic wrap. Allow dough to rest for 30 minutes.

Cut dough into ten even pieces. Using your hands or a rolling pin, stretch each piece of dough into a 5 x 4-inch oval about ¼-inch thick. Make a small hole in the center of each piece. Keep dough covered while all rolling out remaining dough balls.

In a large deep pan, heat 1-inch of oil to 350° F over medium heat. Carefully add 2 to 3 pieces of dough to the hot oil and fry until a light golden brown on each side. Drain on a paper towel lined pan. Serve warm.

FRIED GREEN PLANTAINS

Patacones

4 large green plantains

Salt to taste

Oil for frying

Trim off the ends of each plantain. Cut a slit through the skin along the length of the plantain. Pry off the peel by gradually slipping your fingers between the peel and the plantain. Once peeled, cut crosswise into 1 ½–inch chunks.

Heat oil in a deep fryer or large heavy high–sided pan to 375° F. Working in batches, carefully add plantains to the oil and fry until golden brown and tender, about 5 minutes. Remove from oil to a paper towel–lined sheet and fry remaining plantains.

Place a fried plantain on a board between two pieces of plastic. A zip–top bag works well. Press down firmly to smash the plantain into a 2– to 3–inch round using a glass or the palm of your hand. Repeat the process with the remaining plantains.

Return the plantain slices to the hot oil and fry for an additional 3 to 4 minutes or until golden and crisp. Sprinkle with salt and serve hot.

FISH CEVICHE
Ceviche de Pescado

1 pound boneless, skinless white fish, preferably sea bass or snapper

1 medium onion, finely diced

½ cup finely chopped celery

¼ cup chopped culantro or cilantro

½ teaspoon salt

1 habanero or scotch bonnet pepper, seeds removed and thinly sliced

1 cup fresh lime juice

Cut the fish into small bite–sized pieces and place in a glass bowl. Add the onion, celery, salt, chili pepper, and culantro to the bowl and toss to combine. Pour lime juice over top and mix together carefully. Cover and marinate for 4 at least hours, or until fish becomes opaque.

BAKED SWEET TEMPTATION PLANTAINS

Platanos en Tentación

3 very ripe plantains

½ cup cola

2 tablespoons brown sugar

½ teaspoon ground cinnamon

3 tablespoons butter, cubed

4 – 5 whole cloves

Preheat oven to 350° F. Grease a small baking dish with butter.

Peel the plantains and cut crosswise into 2-inch chunks. Pour cola into pan. Dot each plantain with 1 or 2 pieces of butter. Sprinkle with sugar, cinnamon, and cloves. Bake for 30 – 40 minutes until plantains are soft and golden brown.

PANAMANIAN TORTILLAS

Tortillas Panameñas

14 ounces dried yellow corn

2 tablespoons plus 1 teaspoons salt

Oil for frying

Place corn in a colander and rinse several times under cold running water, removing any debris or stones. Place the corn in a large bowl, cover and let soak overnight.

Drain soaked corn and rinse again. Add to a large pot with 2 tablespoons of salt and add water to cover by 3 to 4 inches. Bring to a boil over medium high–heat, reduce to a simmer and cook for 1 hour or until the corn is softened, stirring occasionally. Add more water as needed to ensure the corn remains covered. To test doneness, place a few kernels of corn on a plate and mash with a fork. Corn that is easily mashed is ready. Drain the corn, reserving 1 cup of cooking liquid.

While corn is still warm, add half to the bowl of a food processor fixed with a steel blade. Add ½ teaspoon of salt. Process mixture until it forms a mostly smooth dough, occasionally stopping to scrape down the bowl and check consistency. The mixture will be very sticky and thick. Pour dough out to a clean surface. Repeat process with remaining dough and ½ teaspoon of salt.

Lightly oil your hands with a small amount of cooking oil to prevent sticking. Begin kneading the prepared dough, adding 1 to 2 tablespoons of cooking liquid to help bring the dough mass together, if needed. Continue kneading until a smooth ball of dough forms. Pat the dough

out into a large circle, about ⅓– to ½–inch thick. Using a 3–inch cookie cutter, cut circles of dough. Carefully lift the dough circles, smoothing any rough edges with your hands. Reroll any remaining dough and repeat the process until all dough has been used.

Heat 2 inches of oil to 350° F in a large deep skillet over medium high heat. Carefully add a few tortillas to the pan and cook on both sides until the yellow color of the tortillas intensifies and begin to lightly brown. Drain on a paper towel lined sheet and season with additional salt, if desired. Repeat with remaining dough circles.

Use a Paila Pot for a traditional experience!

RICE WITH PIGEON PEAS
Arroz con Guandú

1 pound fresh pigeon peas

2 tablespoons extra virgin olive oil

2 teaspoons salt

4 cups white rice, rinsed and drained

Place the pigeon peas in a medium sauce pan. Cover with cold water. Add olive oil and salt. Bring to a boil, reduce heat to a simmer and cook for 15 to 20 minutes.

Add rice to the pot, add more water to cover, stir well and bring to a boil. Once again, reduce heat to low and cook for an additional 15 minutes until liquid has evaporated and rice is tender.

TIP: As a flavorful alternative, replace one cup of water with canned coconut milk when preparing the rice.

The color of the rice will change depending on the depth of color of the pigeon peas. Panama has a very flavorful pigeon pea which colors the rice with a purple-ish hue.

PARTY POTATO SALAD

Ensalada de Feria

2 pounds red or Yukon gold potatoes

2 carrots, peeled and cut into 2 to 3 pieces

3–4 cooked fresh beets chopped in ½–inch pieces (canned cooked beets can also be used)

3 large hard–boiled eggs, roughly chopped

1 small yellow onion, peeled and chopped

2 stalks celery, chopped

1 cup mayonnaise

1 tablespoon yellow mustard

1 tablespoon white vinegar

½ teaspoon salt

¼ teaspoon ground black pepper

Place the potatoes in a large pot and cover with water by 1 inch. Bring the water to a boil and cook until the potatoes are fork tender, about 18 to 20 minutes, adding carrots about halfway through the cooking time. Drain the potatoes and carrots and let them cool slightly. Peel potatoes and cut into 1–inch cubes. Cut carrots in half lengthwise and then cut into ½–inch pieces.

Combine the potatoes and carrots in a large bowl with the eggs, onion, celery and beets. Add mayonnaise, mustard, vinegar, salt and pepper. Stir well to combine. Season with additional salt and pepper or add more mayonnaise as needed.

Refrigerate 3 to 4 hours or until well chilled. Garnish with sliced eggs or chopped parsley.

PANAMANIAN CHICKEN STEW

Sancocho Panameño

1 3 – 3 ½ pound whole chicken, cut into pieces

3 cloves garlic, minced

1 teaspoon dried oregano

1 tablespoon chopped culantro

2 teaspoons salt

1 large onion, chopped

1 pound white ñame, peeled and cut into cubes

1 pound yucca, peeled and cut into cubes

1 pound taro root, peeled and cut into cubes

1 pound fresh pumpkin or calabaza, peeled, seeds removed and cut into cubes

3 ears fresh corn, husked and cut into 2-inch chunks

Place the chicken in a large stock pot and add garlic, oregano, culantro, onion, and salt. Cover with 4 to 6 cups of water. Bring to a boil, reduce heat to low and simmer for 1 hour. Occasionally skim off any impurities that rise to the surface.

Remove chicken from the broth and allow to cool slightly. Add white yam, yucca, and taro root to the pot and simmer for 10 minutes.

Add calabaza and corn to the broth and simmer for an additional 15 to 20 minutes or until all vegetables are tender. While the vegetables cook, debone chicken, cutting meat into bite-size pieces and return to the simmering broth. Season with additional salt and pepper as needed.

TRADITIONAL CHICKEN AND RICE

Arroz con Pollo Tradicional

3 ½ – 4 pound chicken, cut into 8 to 10 pieces

2 tablespoons extra virgin olive oil

3 cups long-grain white rice, rinsed and drained

5 cups chicken broth

1 large onion, diced

2 green bell peppers, diced

2 cloves garlic, minced

8 ounce can tomato sauce

2 tablespoons chopped culantro

8 ounces pimento-stuffed green olives, drained

2 tablespoons capers, drained

1 teaspoon salt

½ teaspoon pepper

1 cup frozen green peas and carrots, thawed

1 small jar diced pimentos

1 banana leaf (optional)

Wash the chicken with water and pat dry. Season chicken with salt and black pepper.

Heat olive oil in a large skillet over medium-high heat. Add chicken to the pan and brown on all sides. Remove from the skillet and set aside.

In the same pan, sauté the onion, peppers and garlic until softened. Reduce heat to low, stir in tomato sauce, culantro, olives, capers, salt, pepper, chicken broth and rice. Add chicken back to the pan, cover with banana leaf (optional) and cook for 15 to 20 minutes until rice is tender and chicken is cooked through.

Remove from heat add peas and carrots; cover to warm through. If desired, remove chicken from the pan and cut into pieces, discarding skin and bones. Add back to the pan and stir to combine. Garnish with diced pimentos and serve.

BEEF EMPANADAS
Empanadas de Carne

1 recipe of prepared Panamanian Tortilla dough (page 22)

1 tablespoon olive oil or achiote oil

½ cup minced onion

½ cup minced green bell pepper

2 cloves garlic, minced

½ pound lean ground beef

1 tablespoon tomato paste

1 tablespoon chopped culantro or cilantro

½ cup green olives, cut in half

1 tablespoon capers

¼ cup dark raisins (optional)

Salt and pepper to taste

Oil for frying

Heat olive oil in a large skillet over medium heat. Add onion, green pepper, and garlic. Season with salt and pepper and sauté until tender, about 5 minutes. Add ground beef, season with salt and pepper, and cook until browned, breaking up any large pieces of ground beef. Stir in the tomato paste, culantro, olives, capers, and raisins, then cook for 2–3 minutes until incorporated. Set aside to cool completely.

Roll pieces of the dough into 2-inch dough balls. Using scissors, cut through the sides of a gallon-sized zip top bag, leaving the bottom of the bag intact. Open the bag and lightly oil the inside of the bag. Place the dough ball in the center of one half of the bag, cover the other half of the bag. Using a plate or other large flat surface, press the dough ball down until it forms a large disc, roughly 6 inches in diameter and a little less than ¼-inch thick.

Add two tablespoons of cooled meat mixture to the center of the dough round. Using the plastic bag, fold the dough over itself, forming a half moon shaped empanada. Firmly seal the edges. Set aside and repeat with remaining dough balls and meat.

Heat 1 inch of oil to 350° F in a large skillet over medium heat. Carefully add 3 to 4 empanadas to the oil and cook for 4 to 5 minutes on each side until the color intensifies to a deep yellow and slightly golden brown color. Drain on paper towel and keep warm while remaining empanadas are fried.

PICKLED PIG'S FEET
Souse

10 pounds split pig feet cut in half and cleaned well

1 tablespoon salt

2 cups freshly squeezed lime juice

5 red habanero or scotch bonnet peppers, seeds removed and sliced very thin

2 large white onions, halved and thinly sliced

4 cucumbers, peeled and thinly sliced

Place the pig's feet in a large stock pot and cover with water. Bring to a boil over high heat, reduce heat and simmer for 30 minutes. Drain, return the pig's feet to the pan and cover with cold water. Bring to a boil, reduce heat and simmer for another 30 minutes. Repeat again, adding fresh water and a tablespoon of salt. Bring to a boil, reduce heat to a simmer and cook for another 20 to 30 minutes, or until just tender and a knife is easily inserted through the skin. Drain, reserving 1 ½ cups of the cooking liquid. Set pigs feet aside to cool.

Add pig's feet to a large bowl with onions, cucumbers, and peppers. Pour cooled cooking liquid and lime juice over top and stir well to combine. Cover and marinate in the refrigerator for a minimum of 5 hours. Serve cold in individual serving bowls.

PANAMANIAN TAMALES

Tamales Panameños

2 pounds dried cracked corn

1 tablespoon hot sauce

3 pound boneless pork shoulder, cut into 5–6 pieces

2 bay leaves

2 large onions, quartered

1 teaspoon dried thyme

2 green bell peppers, cut into large pieces

1 cup dark raisins

4 cloves garlic, minced

1 cup pitted prunes, halved

5–6 culantro leaves

2 cups pimento stuffed olives, drained

2 tablespoons tomato paste

1 cup capers, drained

14 ounce can whole tomatoes, crushed

1 cup frozen peas

¼ cup prepared achiote oil

12 ounces sliced roasted red peppers

2 cups chicken broth

3 packages frozen banana leaves

2 chicken bouillon cubes, if desired

½ cup vegetable oil

Salt and pepper

30 24-inch pieces of cotton twine

Place dried corn in a large container and cover with room temperature water. Soak dried corn for 8 to 12 hours.

Prepare the sofrito by placing onion, green pepper, culantro, garlic, and tomato paste in a food processor or blender and blend until smooth.

Rinse and dry pork and season liberally with salt and pepper. Heat two tablespoons achiote oil in a large pot over medium heat. Brown the meat on all sides. Remove the pork from the pan to a plate. Add sofrito mixture to the pan and cook for 4–5 minutes until softened and slightly reduced. Return meat to the pan along with crushed tomatoes, thyme, bay leaves, chicken stock, bouillon cubes, and hot sauce. Add more chicken stock or water, if needed, to cover. Bring to a simmer, reduce heat to low and cook for 60 to 90 minutes until pork is tender and thoroughly cooked.

Remove pork from the pan and allow to cool slightly. Shred into bite size pieces. Strain the cooking liquid to remove bay leaf and any other large pieces. Add 1 cup of broth to shredded meat and set the remaining broth aside to cool, skimming the fat as it rises to the top.

Drain soaked corn, place in a large stock pot and cover with 3–4 inches of fresh water. Bring to a boil, reduce heat to low and cook, stirring occasionally, until tender, about 45 minutes.

The corn is ready when it mashes easily with a fork. Drain corn and set aside.

While still warm, process corn through a meat grinder, food mill, or a food processer until a smooth dough (masa) has formed. It may be necessary to process the corn twice to obtain a smooth dough. In the bowl of a large mixer add the masa dough along with 1 cup of the pork cooking liquid. Beat with a flat beater on medium speed until well blended and smooth. Continue to add more cooking liquid as needed to reach the desired consistency, being careful not to over moisten the dough. The final dough should be slightly soft, similar to stiff mashed potatoes. Taste for seasoning and add salt, pepper, and additional hot sauce as desired.

Cut 30 pieces of banana leaves into 12 x 12–inch squares. Set aside irregularly sized pieces to be used as patches during the assembly process. Trim off any stems or firm pieces of the leaves. Handle carefully, to avoid any cracks in the leaves. Quickly pass each banana leaf, dull side facing up, over an open flame on the stove to soften the leaves and make them more pliable. This process also enhances the flavor. Set aside.

Place the raisins, prunes, olives, peas, capers, and red pepper in individual bowls to expedite the tamale assembly process.

Place the banana leaf with the dull side facing up. Inspect for cracks and use a piece of reserved banana leaf to patch as needed. Brush each leaf lightly with oil, spreading evenly to coat the center of the banana leaf. Add approximately ¾ cup of masa dough to the center of the banana leaf, spreading evenly to a form a 5 x 5–inch square.

Add a few pieces of meat on the top of the masa square followed by 2 olives, 6 to 8 green peas, capers, a piece of roasted red pepper, and 3 to 4 raisins or 1 to 2 pieces of prunes (or a combination), leaving a 1–inch border of masa on each side. Holding the right and left edges of the banana leaf, bring the left side of the mixture to the center of the leaf, folding the tamale over the top of itself. Repeat from the right–hand side to seal mixture down the center. Repeat from the top and bottom sides of the leaf. The final tamale should be approximately 3 x 3–inches with very little of the filling visible.

Neatly fold the leaves to completely enclose the tamale. Inspect the tamale to ensure there are no cracks or leaks. Carefully wrap the string around the tamale to secure the contents, securing with a knot.

Place a steamer basket in the bottom of a large pot and add enough water to reach the bottom of the basket. Place the 10–12 tamales in the pot on top of the steamer basket. Bring to a boil, reduce heat to medium low and cook for 25 to 30 minutes. Repeat with remaining tamales. Set aside to cool slightly before serving. To freeze tamales, use a vacuum sealer or wrap each tamal individually in plastic wrap then aluminum foil and store in a freezer bag.

TIP: If you are making tamales with different meats, to distinguish them apart once finished, cut strings made out of banana leaf and make a knot on one type of the tamales.

QUEEN'S BITE CAKE
Bocado de la Reina

CAKE

4 eggs, separated

⅔ cups granulated sugar

1 teaspoon vanilla extract

1 cup all-purpose flour

1 teaspoon baking powder

1/8 teaspoon salt

SYRUP

3 cups sugar

3 cups water

20 pitted prunes

½ cup dark raisins

2 cinnamon sticks

6 whole cloves

½ cup dark Panamanian rum

⅓ cup dry or sweet sherry

½ cup pearl sugar

Preheat the oven to 350° F. Lightly grease an 8 or 9-inch square baking pan.

Combine flour, baking soda, and salt in a small bowl. In another bowl, beat the egg yolks with the sugar and vanilla until light and fluffy. In a separate mixing bowl, beat egg whites on high speed until stiff peaks form. Fold in the beaten egg mixture. Once combined, fold in the flour mixture, being sure to scrape the bottom of the bowl to fully incorporate the dry ingredients. Pour the mixture into the prepared pan.

Bake for 18 to 20 minutes or until a skewer inserted into the center comes out clean. Remove from oven and cool on a wire rack.

While the cake cools, prepare the rum syrup. In a saucepan, combine sugar, water, cinnamon sticks, cloves, prunes, and raisins. Bring to a boil over high heat, stir until sugar is dissolved. Reduce heat to low and cook for 7 to 8 minutes. Remove from heat and add the dark rum and sherry. Cool for 30 minutes and remove the cinnamon sticks and cloves.

Remove cake from the pan, cut into 16 to 20 squares and arrange on a serving platter. Pour syrup over top and decorate with the prunes, raisins, and pearl sugar.

BEVERAGES

CRANBERRY MOCKTAIL
Cóctel sin Alcohol de Arándanos

4 cups cranberry juice cocktail

½ cup freshly squeezed lime juice

6 cups ginger ale

Frozen cranberries and lime slices for garnish

Combine cranberry juice and lime juice together in a pitcher. Chill until cold.

Add ginger ale just before serving.

Rim the glasses with lime juice then roll in granulated sugar. Serve over ice and garnish with cranberries and lime slices.

BEACH PARTY PUNCH
Ponche de Fiesta de Playa

12 ounces orange juice concentrate

14 ounces passion fruit pulp

3 cups water

46 ounce can pineapple juice

½ cup freshly squeezed lime juice

6 cups club soda

Orange slices, lime slices, and maraschino cherries for garnish

Combine orange juice, passion fruit pulp, and water together in a large pitcher or punch bowl. Add pineapple juice and lime juice and mix well. Chill until cold.

Add club soda just before serving. Serve over ice and garnish with fruit.

SANGRIA
Sangría

1 lemon, cut into slices

1 orange, cut into slices

1 lime, cut into slices

6 strawberries, halved

1 green apple, cored and chopped

1 bottle pinot noir

¼ cup brandy, bourbon or rum

1 cup simple syrup

2 cups club soda

Add all ingredients except club soda to a pitcher. Stir to combine well. Refrigerate 12 hours. Add club soda just before serving. Serve over ice and garnish with additional slices of citrus, if desired.

PANAMANIAN TROPICAL COCKTAIL
Chichita Panameña

1 750 ml bottle Seco Herrerano or white rum

2 46–ounce cans pineapple juice

2 46–ounce cans grapefruit juice

1 to 2 cups simple syrup, to taste

5 drops bitters

Combine all ingredients together in a large pitcher or punch bowl. Refrigerate until cold.

Serve over ice and garnish with citrus slices or pineapple wedges.

CELEBRATION EGG NOG

Ron Ponche

1 750 ml bottle of Panamanian dark rum

12 large eggs, separated

4 14–ounce cans sweetened condensed milk

5 12–ounce cans evaporated milk

3 tablespoons vanilla extract

Grated fresh nutmeg to taste (optional)

Beat the egg whites together in a large mixing bowl until stiff peaks form. Set aside.

In another large bowl, beat 6 egg yolks with half of the condensed milk and half of the evaporated milk until well combined. Mix in the remaining egg yolks and milks. Add the rum and beat until well mixed. Gently fold in the reserved egg whites until the mixture is light and fluffy and egg whites have been completely incorporated.

Refrigerate at least 12 hours before serving, stirring occasionally. Pour mixture into individual bottles or a large punch bowl and top with grated nutmeg before serving.

SAUCES & ACCOMPANIMENTS

ACHIOTE OIL
Aceite de Achiote

½ cup vegetable oil or olive oil

1 tablespoon achiote seeds

Place oil and achiote seeds in a small saucepan over medium–low heat. Cook for 5 to 7 minutes, stirring occasionally, until the achiote seeds have released their color and the oil has become a deep red color. Do not overheat the oil as the achiote seeds will become black and ruin the oil.

Strain oil into a heatproof glass jar or bowl. Refrigerate oil for up to one week.

SOFRITO
Sofrito

4 cloves garlic

8 culantro leaves

1 large white onion, peeled and quartered

1 green bell pepper, core removed and cut into pieces

1 red bell pepper, core removed and cut into pieces

¼ cup tomato paste

¼ cup achiote oil

1 teaspoon salt

½ teaspoon black pepper

Add the garlic and culantro to the bowl of a food processor fitted with a steel blade. Pulse several times until garlic and culantro are finely minced. Add the onion and bell peppers and process until a smooth paste forms. Add the remaining ingredients and process until combined.

Use immediately or store refrigerated in an air-tight container for 7 to 10 days.

TIP: To freeze, place small portions of the sofrito in an ice cube tray. Frozen cubes can be stored in a freezer bag for up to 6 months.

FRESH SALSA
Salsa Fresca

6 to 7 Roma tomatoes, cored, seeded and chopped

1 medium white onion, chopped

½ cup chopped cilantro leaves and stems

1 jalapeno pepper, seeded and minced (optional)

1 lime, juiced

Salt to taste

Add tomato, onion, cilantro, and jalapeno to a bowl. Stir to combine. Add lime juice and season with salt. Cover and refrigerate for one hour before serving.

MANGO SALSA
Salsa de Mango

1 to 2 large ripe mangoes, peeled, pitted, and diced

¼ cup chopped red onion

1 clove garlic, minced

2 tablespoons chopped cilantro

1 jalapeno pepper, minced (optional)

1/3 cup fresh lime juice

Salt and pepper to taste

Combine all ingredients together in a small bowl and stir to combine. Season with salt and pepper. Cover and refrigerate for one hour before serving. Spoon over grilled chicken or serve with tortilla chips.

BALSAMIC VINAIGRETTE
Vinagre Balsámico

¼ cup balsamic vinegar

½ cup extra virgin olive oil

½ teaspoon Dijon mustard

1 clove garlic, grated

½ teaspoon dried basil or oregano

Salt and pepper to taste

Combine all ingredients together in a jar with a tight–fitting lid. Shake well to combine. Adjust seasoning to taste. Shake again before serving. Delicious served over a green salad or used as a marinade.

GREEN VINAIGRETTE
Salsa Verde

1 tablespoon white vinegar

2 tablespoons fresh lime juice

3 tablespoons extra virgin olive oil

¼ teaspoon Tabasco sauce

3 tablespoons chopped parsley

3 tablespoons chopped chives

1 tablespoon chopped dill pickles

1 tablespoon chopped green pepper

Combine all ingredients in a blender or food processor until thick and emulsified. Serve over a garden salad or use as a fresh sauce over grilled meat or fish.

HOMEMADE MAYONNAISE
Salsa de Mayonesa Domestica

2 large egg yolks at room temperature

1 teaspoon salt

½ teaspoon granulated sugar

2 tablespoons lemon juice

1 teaspoon Dijon mustard

¼ teaspoon paprika

¾ cups extra–virgin olive oil

In a blender or food processor, blend together the egg, lemon juice, mustard, salt, sugar, and paprika, blending until well combined. With the motor still running, add the oil in a very slow, thin, steady stream and blend until the dressing is thick and smooth.

The mayonnaise can be prepared ahead and refrigerated in an airtight container up to one week.

CHIMICHURRI SAUCE
Salsa Chimichurri

½ cup olive oil

¼ cup red wine vinegar

½ cup chopped cilantro

½ cup finely diced onion

4 cloves garlic, minced

1 tablespoon chopped parsley (optional)

Salt and black pepper to taste

Combine all ingredients together in a small bowl. Cover and refrigerate for 2 to 3 hours before serving.

Delicious served with steaks, chicken or seafood.

The Chimichurri sauce is great for dipping fried yucca or patacones!

APPETIZERS & SALADS

PIZZA BITES
Pizzitas Caseras

1 French baguette, cut diagonally into 1–inch thick slices

½ cup butter

1 cup prepared pizza or marinara sauce

2 cups shredded mozzarella cheese

½ cup grated Parmesan cheese

6 ounces sliced pepperoni

Salt and black pepper

Preheat oven to 375° F.

Lightly butter one side of the baguette slices and place on a rimmed baking sheet. Add a tablespoon of pizza sauce followed by a sprinkling of mozzarella and Parmesan cheese. Add two slices of pepperoni to the top of each piece of baguette.

Bake for 10 to 15 minutes, until cheese is melted and bubbling. Cool slightly before serving.

MARINATED MUSHROOMS
Hongos Marinados

28–ounce can whole mushrooms, drained

1 medium onion, finely chopped

3 cloves garlic, minced

½ cup apple cider vinegar

½ cup cold water

½ cup extra virgin olive oil

Salt and pepper to taste

Add mushrooms, onion, and garlic to a medium bowl. In another bowl, stir together vinegar, water, and olive oil until well combined. Pour over the mushroom mixture and stir well. Season with salt and pepper.

Marinate for 4 hours or overnight before serving.

BACON-WRAPPED PRUNES
Ciruelas Pasas Envueltas en Tocino

1 pound thinly sliced smoked bacon, cut in half

30 to 36 pitted prunes

½ cup dulce de leche or goat cheese

Preheat oven to 375° F. Line a baking sheet with parchment paper.

Fill each prune with a rounded teaspoonful of dulce de leche or goat cheese and reseal. Wrap each prune with a half piece of bacon. Secure bacon with a decorative toothpick and place on the baking sheet. Repeat with remaining prunes and bacon.

Bake for 15 to 20 minutes or until bacon is crisp. Remove from baking sheet to a serving platter. Serve warm or at room temperature.

CHEESE STRAWS
Palitroques de Queso

½ cup butter

1 cup grated sharp cheddar cheese

1 cup all-purpose flour, sifted

½ teaspoon salt

¼ teaspoon black pepper

¼ teaspoon cayenne pepper (optional)

Preheat oven to 350° F. Line two baking sheets with parchment paper. Set aside.

In a large bowl, beat butter until light and fluffy. Beat in cheese until blended. Combine flour, salt, and pepper; stir into cheese mixture until a dough forms. Roll into a 15 x 6-inch rectangle. Cut into 30 six-inch strips. Gently place strips 1 inch apart on prepared baking sheets.

Bake until lightly browned, 15 to 20 minutes. Cool 5 minutes before removing from pans to wire racks to cool completely. Store in an airtight container.

TROPICAL FRUIT SALAD
Cóctel de Frutas Tropicales

1 small papaya, peeled and seeded

1 pineapple, peeled and cored

2 grapefruit, peeled

6 oranges, peeled

1 lime

½ cup granulated sugar

Cut the papaya into 1-inch pieces. Cut the grapefruit and oranges crosswise into ½-inch slices, then cut into quarters. Place the fruits into a large serving bowl. Add the zest and juice of the lime with the granulated sugar. Stir well to combine. Adjust sugar as needed. Refrigerate for 2 hours before serving.

COLESLAW WITH PINEAPPLE
Ensalada de Repollo con Piña

2 tablespoons white vinegar

¼ cup extra virgin olive oil

½ teaspoon black pepper

½ teaspoon salt

1 teaspoon sugar

2 cups sliced cabbage or coleslaw mix

1 cup diced fresh pineapple

In a small jar, combine vinegar, olive oil, black pepper, salt, and sugar. Shake well to combine. Set aside.

Place cabbage and pineapple in a medium bowl. Add prepared dressing and mix well. Refrigerate for 2 to 3 hours before serving to allow flavors to meld.

GREEN MANGO SALAD
Ensalada de Mango Verde

3 to 4 firm large green mangoes

½ small sweet onion, thinly sliced

¼ cup extra virgin olive oil

1 tablespoon apple cider vinegar

1 tablespoon water

Salt and pepper

Hot sauce

Chopped cilantro or parsley for garnish

Peel mangoes, cut flesh away from the pit and cut into ¼-inch slices. Add to a bowl with the onion.

In a small bowl, combine the olive oil, vinegar, and water. Season with hot sauce, salt, and pepper to taste. Pour over the mango and onion mixture and stir to combine.

Cover and refrigerate for 2 to 3 hours before serving to allow flavors to combine.

Garnish with chopped cilantro or parsley, if desired.

SIDE DISHES

PARMESAN POTATO GRATIN

Papas Gratinadas a la Parmesana

5 to 6 large baking potatoes

12 ounces evaporated milk

1 ½ cups water

2 teaspoons kosher salt

½ teaspoon black pepper

1 cup freshly grated Parmesan cheese

4 tablespoons butter

Preheat oven to 375° F. Coat a 13 x 9–inch baking dish with a thin layer of cooking spray or butter.

Mix together the evaporated milk, water, salt, and black pepper in a pitcher. Wash, peel, and very thinly slice the potatoes using a potato peeler or mandolin.

Place half of the potatoes in a single layer in the baking dish. Dot the top with 2 tablespoons of butter followed by ¼ cup of Parmesan cheese sprinkled evenly over the top. Add the remaining potatoes to the top in an even layer. Pour the milk mixture evenly over the top. Dot the top of the potatoes with 2 tablespoons butter and sprinkle with remaining Parmesan cheese.

Bake for 1 hour or until the potatoes are tender and a golden brown crust has formed.

SWEET AND SAVORY PLANTAINS
Platanos Dulces y Salados

3 very ripe plantains

2 tablespoons butter, cubed

½ cup honey

2 tablespoons grated Parmesan cheese

Preheat oven to 350° F. Lightly coat a 13 x 9–inch baking dish with butter.

Peel plantains and slice in half lengthwise. Place in the baking dish. Place butter cubes over the plantains. Drizzle with honey then sprinkle Parmesan cheese evenly over the top.

Bake for 20 to 30 minutes, until plantains have softened and browned.

SWEET POTATO CASSEROLE
Caserola de Papas Dulces

4 large sweet potatoes

8 ounces crushed pineapple, drained

½ cup packed brown sugar

¼ cup butter

½ teaspoon salt

1 teaspoon ground cinnamon

2 cups miniature marshmallows

Preheat oven to 400° F.

Pierce each sweet potato several times with a knife or fork. Place on a rimmed baking sheet lined with parchment paper. Bake until tender, about 45 minutes.

Reduce oven to 350° F. Coat a casserole dish with butter or cooking spray.

Cut the potatoes in half lengthwise, scoop out the flesh and place in a mixing bowl. Discard the potato skins. Mash the potatoes until mostly smooth, some small lumps are fine. Add the butter, brown sugar, salt, cinnamon, and pineapple and mix together until well combined.

Transfer mixture to a greased 2–quart baking dish. Top with an even layer of marshmallows.

Bake until center is warmed through and marshmallows are lightly browned, about 15 to 20 minutes.

WARM GREEN BEAN SALAD
Ensalada de Habichuelas con Cebollas

1 pound fresh green beans

1 medium red onion, sliced

¼ cup sliced almonds

2 tablespoons extra virgin olive oil

3 tablespoons apple cider vinegar

Salt and black pepper to taste

Clean and trim the green beans. Bring a large pot of water to a boil and season with salt. Add green beans and cook for 5–7 minutes, or until crisp but tender. Drain and set aside.

Add the sliced almonds to a large pan set over medium heat. Toast almonds for 3 to 4 minutes, until lightly golden. Remove from pan and set aside.

In the same pan, heat the olive oil over medium heat. Add onions and sauté until softened and lightly golden, about 8 to 10 minutes. Add green beans and cook for another 4 to 5 minutes. Add vinegar to the pan and season with salt and pepper. Stir well to combine.

Remove to a serving bowl or platter and sprinkle with toasted almonds. Serve warm.

CHEESE SOUFFLÉ
Soufflé de Queso

2 tablespoons butter

2 tablespoons all-purpose flour

½ teaspoon salt

⅛ teaspoon black pepper

1 cup whole milk

1 cup water

8 ounces sharp cheddar cheese, grated

3 large eggs, separated

1 teaspoon baking powder

Preheat oven to 400° F. Butter a 6-cup soufflé dish.

Melt butter in a medium saucepan over low heat. Whisk in flour, salt, and pepper until a smooth paste forms. Slowly whisk in milk until well combined. Add water. Bring to a simmer and cook for 4 to 5 minutes, or until thickened. Add cheddar cheese, stirring until well combined. Remove from heat and add egg yolks one at a time, whisking to blend after each addition. Stir in baking powder. Scrape soufflé base into a large bowl and allow to cool until lukewarm.

Using an electric mixer, beat egg whites in another large bowl until stiff, but not dry. Fold one quarter of the whites into the soufflé base to loosen the mixture. Fold in remaining whites in 2 batches. Transfer the batter to the prepared dish and smooth out the top.

Place dish in the oven and immediately reduce oven temperature to 375° F. Bake until soufflé is puffed and golden brown on top and center moves only slightly with the dish is shaken gently, about 25 minutes (do not open the oven door during the first 20 minutes).

Serve immediately.

CARROT SOUFFLÉ
Soufflé de Zanahoria

8 large carrots, peeled and cut into 1-inch chunks

1 12-ounce can evaporated milk

2 large eggs

¼ cup granulated sugar

Butter for dish

Bring a large pot of water to a boil. Add carrots and cook until tender, about 15 minutes. Drain and cool. Place carrots in the bowl of a food processor and blend until smooth.

Preheat oven to 300° F. Butter a soufflé dish.

Combine carrots, evaporated milk, eggs, and sugar together in a large mixing bowl. Pour mixture into the prepared dish. Bake for 30 minutes or until a knife inserted into the center comes out clean.

Serve immediately.

PASTA WITH BASIL PESTO
Pasta con Pesto

2 cups loosely packed basil leaves

3 to 4 cloves garlic, peeled

8 ounces Feta cheese, crumbled

½ cup extra virgin olive oil

Salt and black pepper to taste

1 pound linguine, spaghetti or fusilli

Prepare pasta according to package directions.

While pasta cooks, combine the basil, garlic, Feta cheese, and olive oil together in a food processor until smooth. Season with salt and pepper.

Drain pasta, reserving ¼ cup of pasta water. Return the pasta to the pan, add the pesto sauce and pasta water and stir to combine.

Garnish with additional Feta cheese and basil leaves, if desired.

HUANCAÍNA PERUVIAN POTATO SALAD
Papas a la Huancaína

2 pounds Yukon gold potatoes, peeled

2 medium onions, thinly sliced into rounds

1 cup lime juice

1 cup water

¼ cup extra virgin olive oil

1 pound Feta cheese, crumbled

3 cups whole milk

¼ Habanero pepper or yellow pepper (optional)

6 eggs, boiled, peeled and sliced

1 cup Kalamata olives, halved

Iceberg lettuce leaves

Boil potatoes in a large pot of salted water until slightly firm, but tender when pierced with a tip of a knife. Do not overcook. Drain and set aside to cool. Sliced cooled potatoes into half–inch rounds.

In a medium bowl, stir together olive oil, lime juice, and water. Add onions to the mixture. Set aside to marinate.

Warm the milk in a saucepan set over medium heat. Add Feta cheese and the pepper and cook until hot and cheese has softened. If desired, place the mixture in a blender and process until smooth and cool.

To serve, place a bed of lettuce leaves on a large platter followed by a layer of sliced potatoes. Pour cheese sauce over top. Decorate with drained onions, sliced eggs, and Kalamata olives.

COCONUT RICE WITH RAISINS
Arroz con Coco y Pasas

3 cups white rice

2 tablespoons brown sugar

2 ¼ cups coconut milk

2 ¼ cups cola

4 tablespoons butter

1 ½ tablespoons salt

1 cup dark raisins

Rinse rice under cold water until water runs clear. Set aside to drain completely.

Melt butter in a medium saucepan over medium heat. Add raisins and sauté until raisins soften and begin to burst. Add the brown sugar and stir to combine. Add rice and sauté until coated with butter and rice has turned opaque. Stir in coconut milk, cola, and salt and bring to a simmer. Reduce heat to low, cover and cook for 15–20 minutes, or until rice is tender, being careful not to scorch. Fluff rice with a fork and serve immediately.

GOLDEN VERMICELLI RICE
Arroz con Fideos

2 tablespoons butter or extra virgin olive oil

1 cup fine vermicelli noodles, fideos, or broken angel hair pasta

1 garlic clove, minced

2 cups rice, rinsed and drained

3 cups chicken stock

1 teaspoon salt

1 tablespoon finely minced parsley (optional)

Melt butter in a heavy bottomed pot over medium heat. Add noodles and cook until they begin to toast and turn a light golden brown. Add the garlic and cook for 1 minute. Add the rice and stir, coating the grains with butter. Cook until the rice is translucent and has a light toasty aroma. Add the chicken stock and salt, stir well, then bring to a boil.

Reduce heat to low; cover and cook for 12 to 15 minutes until all liquid has absorbed and rice is tender. Remove from heat, add chopped parsley, fluff with a fork and serve.

RED KIDNEY BEANS & RICE
Arroz con Porotos

1 pound dried kidney beans

4 slices bacon

1 green bell pepper, chopped

1 medium yellow onion, chopped

2 cloves garlic, minced

8 leaves culantro, chopped

1–2 cups sliced cooked smoked sausage (optional)

6 cups chicken broth or water

8 ounce can tomato sauce

Salt and pepper

Hot sauce to taste

Prepared white rice for serving

Place beans in a large bowl and soak in 8 cups of water overnight. Drain beans, rinse with cold water and set aside.

In a large pot, cook bacon until just crisp. Remove from the pan to drain. Add green bell pepper and onion to the pan with the bacon fat over medium heat. Cook for 4 to 5 minutes until vegetables are softened slightly. Add garlic and cook for 1 minute. Add beans to the pan with culantro, chicken broth, tomato sauce, and smoked sausage. Add additional water, if needed, to have enough liquid to cover the beans by 2 inches.

Bring to a boil. Reduce to a simmer, and cook until tender, about 30 minutes. About 15 minutes before the beans are done, add salt, pepper, and hot sauce to taste.

Serve with prepared white rice.

MAIN COURSES

SHRIMP SCAMPI

Camarones al Ajillo

1 pound large shrimp, peeled and deveined

2 tablespoons butter

2 tablespoons extra virgin olive oil

4 cloves garlic, minced

1 teaspoon dried Italian seasoning

½ cup dry white wine

½ teaspoon red pepper flakes

½ teaspoon kosher salt

2 tablespoons chopped flat leaf parsley

1 tablespoon fresh lemon juice

Lemon wedges for garnish

In a large skillet over medium–high heat, melt butter and olive oil. Add garlic and Italian seasoning and sauté for 1 minute. Add white wine, red pepper flakes, and salt. Cook for 2 to 3 minutes or until wine is reduced by half.

Add shrimp and sauté just until they turn pink, about 3 to 4 minutes. Stir in the lemon juice and parsley.

Serve with pasta of choice or with a crusty loaf of bread.

SHRIMP FRIED RICE

Arroz Frito Chino con Camarones

1 pound medium-sized shrimp, peeled and deveined

2 tablespoons vegetable oil, divided

1 egg, beaten

¾ cup diced ham

¾ cup sliced white mushrooms (optional)

½ cup minced onion

2 green onions, chopped

1 teaspoon toasted sesame oil

2 cups cold day-old steamed white rice

½ cup frozen peas, thawed

1 teaspoon dark soy sauce

1 tablespoon light soy sauce

Have all ingredients prepped and ready before beginning the cooking process.

Heat one tablespoon of oil in a large skillet over medium-high heat. Add shrimp, season with salt and pepper and sauté until cooked through. Remove from skillet to a plate to keep warm. Add beaten egg to the pan and spread into a single thin layer. Cook and remove from pan, slice into thin strips; set aside with shrimp.

Add the remaining tablespoon of oil to the pan followed by ham, mushrooms, and onions. Cook until onions are softened. Add sesame oil to the pan followed by the rice. Cook for 5 minutes, until the rice is warmed through. Season with soy sauces. Stir in peas, shrimp and egg; cook until all ingredients are warm. Add more soy sauce to taste.

STEAMED CLAMS IN GARLIC SAUCE

Almejas al Ajillo

2 tablespoons olive oil

3 cloves garlic, minced

1 teaspoon dried red pepper flakes

½ teaspoon salt

36 littleneck clams, scrubbed and drained

1 cup dry white wine

1 tablespoon chopped fresh parsley

Lemon wedges

Heat olive oil over medium–high heat in a deep-sided skillet with a tight-fitting lid. Add garlic, salt, and red pepper flakes and cook until garlic turns a pale golden brown, about 4 to 5 minutes. Increase the heat to high, add clams and white wine. Cover the pan and cook, shaking the pan occasionally, until all the clams are open.

Remove from the heat, sprinkle with parsley. Season the sauce with additional salt and pepper, if needed. Serve the clams with sauce and lemon wedges.

BAKED SALMON
Salmón al Horno

4 center-cut salmon filets,
6 to 7 ounces each

¼ cup drained capers

½ cup dry white wine

1 tablespoon lemon juice

2 cloves garlic, minced

2 tablespoons butter

Salt and black pepper to taste

2 tablespoons chopped parsley or dill
(optional)

Additional lemon wedges for serving

Preheat oven to 350° F. Spray a baking dish with non-stick cooking spray.

Place filets skin side down in a baking dish. Season with salt and black pepper. Top each filet with ½ tablespoon of butter, chopped garlic, and capers. Pour white wine and lemon juice around the filets. Bake for 15 to 20 minutes, or until desired doneness.

Sprinkle with chopped herbs and a squeeze of fresh lemon before serving. Spoon sauce over top, if desired.

MARINATED FISH
Escabeche de Pescado

1 pound white fish filets, preferably bass or snapper

½ cup all-purpose flour

1 teaspoon salt

½ teaspoon black pepper

½ teaspoon garlic powder

1 cup extra virgin olive oil

1 medium onion, sliced into rings

1 green bell pepper, sliced into rings

1 habanero pepper, seeds removed and thinly sliced

½ cup red wine vinegar

½ cup pimento stuffed olives

1 bay leaf

¾ cup water

Salt and pepper to taste

In small saucepan over medium-high heat, bring vinegar, onion, olives, bay leaf, habanero pepper, and water. Reduce heat. Simmer, stirring occasionally, until onions are soft, about 10 minutes; set aside to cool.

Mix together flour, salt, pepper and garlic powder. Toss fish filets with flour mixture, patting off excess. Heat olive oil in medium skillet over medium high heat. Add fish. Cook, turning once, until fish is golden brown on both sides and cooked through, about 5 to 6 minutes. Transfer fish to a glass baking dish.

Pour reserved sauce over fish; cover with plastic wrap. Refrigerate at least 24 hours, or up to 48 hours. Serve cold.

SPICY PORK CHOPS
Chuletas Picantes

4 bone–in pork chops, about ¾–inch thick

½ teaspoon salt

¼ teaspoon black pepper

1 tablespoon vegetable oil

2 cloves garlic, minced

2 cups prepared salsa (mild to medium)

2 tablespoons chopped cilantro or culantro

½ cup small pimento stuffed green olives

2 tablespoons drained capers

½ cup water

Season pork chops on both sides with salt and pepper.

Heat vegetable oil over medium heat in a large skillet with a tight fitting lid. Add pork chops. Sauté for 3 to 4 minutes on each side until lightly golden. Add garlic, salsa, cilantro, olives, capers, and water. Cover and cook for 20 to 30 minutes over low heat until pork chops are tender.

Serve with rice, pasta or potatoes.

POTATO CASSEROLE WITH HAM

Cazuela de Papas con Jamón

2 pounds of russet potatoes, washed, peeled and thinly sliced

½ pound cooked ham, diced

1 large onion, peeled and thinly sliced

4 tablespoons butter, cubed

1 cup whole milk

1 tablespoon all-purpose flour

Salt and black pepper

Preheat oven to 350° F. Grease a 13 x 9–inch baking dish with butter.

Place one third of the potatoes in the bottom of the baking dish. Top with half of the ham and onion followed by one tablespoon of butter. Sprinkle with salt, pepper, and half of the flour. Repeat for a second layer. Place the remaining potatoes on top and pour milk evenly over the casserole. Season the potatoes with salt and pepper and dot the top with remaining two tablespoons of butter.

Cover with aluminum foil and bake for 45 minutes. Remove foil and cook for another 15 minutes until the top is golden brown.

RICE WITH PORK AND VEGETABLES
Arroz con Puerco y Vegetales

1 pound pork shoulder, cubed and trimmed of excess fat

2 teaspoons adobo seasoning

2 tablespoons vegetable oil

1 teaspoon salt

½ teaspoon black pepper

3 tablespoons sliced green onions

1 cup diced celery

2 green bell peppers, seeded and chopped

1 large onion, halved and sliced

2 medium tomatoes, chopped

1 carrot, peeled and grated

1 cup frozen green beans, thawed

2 cups long-grain white rice

8 ounces tomato sauce

1 tablespoon Worcestershire sauce

2 cups water

Season pork with adobo. Heat 2 tablespoons oil in a large skillet over medium-high heat. Add pork cubes and cook until browned on all sides. Drain and set aside.

To the same pan, add green onions, celery, green peppers, and onion. Season with salt and black pepper. Sauté for 4 to 5 minutes until vegetables begin to soften. Add tomato, carrot and green beans. Stir to combine. Add rice and cook for 5 minutes. Add tomato sauce, Worcestershire sauce, and water. Stir well. Cover and cook for 15 to 20 minutes, until liquid has been absorbed and rice is tender.

ROAST LEG OF PORK
Pernil de Puerco

1 (14 – 16 pound) bone-in whole pork leg

½ cup extra virgin olive oil

2 tablespoons annatto seeds

8 cloves garlic, finely minced

1 tablespoon kosher salt

1 teaspoon black pepper

2 teaspoons ground cumin

1 tablespoon dried oregano

½ cup white vinegar, lime juice or sour orange juice

Combine olive oil and annatto seeds in a small saucepan and cook over medium-low heat for 4 to 5 minutes until oil turns dark red, being careful not to burn the annatto seeds. Remove from heat, drain into a heatproof bowl, discarding annatto seeds. Set aside to cool.

Combine cooled oil, garlic, salt, pepper, cumin, oregano, and vinegar together in a small bowl. Set aside.

Wash the pork leg and pat dry. With a sharp knife, cut small slits all over the pork leg. Place the pork in a large roasting pan and rub the prepared oil mixture all over the pork leg, pushing the mixture into the open slits. Cover and marinate for at least 4 hours or overnight.

Preheat oven to 350° F.

Roast for 5 to 6 hours, basting with pan juices every hour until the skin is a crispy golden brown. Remove from the oven, cover loosely with aluminum foil and allow to rest for 20 to 30 minutes before carving.

Prepare a pan sauce with the drippings, if desired.

EGGPLANT LASAGNA WITH PORK RAGU

Lasagna de Berenjena con Puerco

2 large eggplants, sliced ½–inch thick (about 8 slices)

5 tablespoons extra virgin olive oil

1 pound ground pork

1 teaspoon salt

½ teaspoon black pepper

1 large onion, chopped

3 large tomatoes, chopped

1 large bell pepper, chopped

2 cloves garlic, peeled and minced

3 tablespoons tomato paste

2 cups fresh or frozen thawed sweet corn

1 cup grated Parmesan cheese

Salt and black pepper to taste

Preheat oven to 400° F.

Arrange sliced eggplant in a single layer on 2 sheet pans. Brush on both sides with 3 tablespoons olive oil and season with salt and pepper. Roast the eggplant until it is soft and golden, about 25 minutes. Turn slices halfway through cooking.

While eggplant cooks, heat 2 tablespoons olive oil in a large skillet over medium heat. Add ground pork and season with salt and pepper. Break up large pieces and cook until browned. Add onion, tomatoes, bell peppers, and garlic and cook until vegetables are softened, about 10 minutes. Stir in tomato paste and corn and cook for 5 more minutes. Set aside to cool slightly.

Reduce oven to 350° F.

Brush an 8-inch baking dish with olive oil. Spread ¼ of the meat sauce on bottom of the prepared baking dish. Lay 2–3 eggplant slices on top followed by ¼ of the meat sauce mixture and ¼ cup of Parmesan. Repeat. Top with the remaining ¼ cup meat mixture and remaining Parmesan cheese. Bake until golden brown, at 350° F, for 30 minutes.

BABY BACK RIBS WITH WHISKEY SAUCE
Costillas al Whiskey

2 racks of baby back ribs, about 4 pounds

1 cup prepared smoky barbecue sauce

⅓ cup whiskey

⅓ cup ketchup

⅓ cup brown sugar

3 tablespoons vegetable oil

3 tablespoons Worcestershire sauce

½ small onion, grated

2 cloves garlic, minced

½ teaspoon fresh minced ginger

1 teaspoon yellow mustard

Salt and pepper

Cut each rack of ribs in half and season with salt and pepper. Spread barbecue sauce over the ribs. Place ribs in a plastic zip top bag and marinate for 24 hours.

Add whiskey, ketchup, brown sugar, oil, Worcestershire sauce, onion, garlic, ginger, and mustard to a medium saucepan and stir well. Simmer over medium low heat for 10 minutes. Remove from heat and cool.

Remove ribs from the refrigerator and bring to room temperature, about one hour before cooking. Preheat oven to 350° F. Place ribs, meat side up, on an aluminum foil lined baking sheet that has been coated with cooking spray. Brush ribs with a layer of whiskey sauce. Roast for 75 minutes, or until the meat easily pulls away from the bones. Baste with the whiskey sauce twice during baking.

Serve with remaining sauce on the side.

STUFFED LOIN OF BEEF
Lomo Relleno

3 pound eye of round roast

½ pound thinly sliced bacon

15 pitted green olives

10 pitted prunes

3 cloves garlic, mashed

1 large onion, sliced into thick rounds

1 bay leaf

1 cup dry red wine

¼ cup brown sugar

Salt and black pepper

Preheat oven to 400° F.

Use a long, sharp knife to pierce a hole in center of both ends of loin. Working from both ends, use handle of a large wooden spoon to force a cavity all the way through center of loin. Remove spoon and push handle through several more times, widening the cavity. Working with a few prunes and olives, push them into the cavity with your fingers and spoon handle. Work from both ends until cavity is stuffed from end to end. Rub the exterior of the loin with the mashed garlic and season with salt and pepper.

Wrap the loin in bacon slices and place in a roasting pan. Add sliced onions, bay leaf and 2 cups of water to the pan. Roast for 1 hour, adding more water as needed to prevent scorching.

Remove from oven and allow beef to rest on a carving board lightly covered with aluminum foil for 15 to 20 minutes. Return the pan to the stove top, add wine and brown sugar, bring to a simmer and cook until the sauce is reduced and thickened slightly. Slice the beef and place on a platter. Serve sauce over top or on the side.

ITALIAN SPAGHETTI AND MEATBALLS

Bolas de Carne a la Italiana

1 pound lean ground beef

3 slices white bread, crusts removed and cubed

¼ cup milk

1 medium onion, grated

1 clove garlic, minced

1 medium tomato, chopped

1 large green pepper, seeded and finely chopped

1 egg

1 teaspoon salt

½ teaspoon black pepper

Prepared marinara sauce

1 pound spaghetti or rigatoni

Preheat oven to 400° F. Line a large baking sheet with parchment paper or aluminum foil sprayed with cooking spray.

In a large bowl, mix all ingredients together just until combined. Do not overwork the mixture. Shape into 24 meatballs and place 1-inch apart on the prepared baking sheet. Bake for 20 to 25 minutes.

Add meatballs to prepared marinara sauce and simmer for 20 minutes. Cook pasta according to package directions. Serve meatballs and sauce over top of the pasta.

NOTE: As an alternative to baking, meatballs may be fried until golden brown in a large sauté pan with ¼ cup olive oil.

BEEF AND BEAN CHILI
Chili con Carne

1 pound lean ground beef

1 ½ teaspoons kosher salt

½ teaspoon ground black pepper

2 tablespoons chili powder

1 large onion, finely chopped

1 large green bell pepper, finely chopped

1 stalk celery, minced

2 cloves garlic, minced

14 ounce can kidney beans, rinsed and drained

14 ounce can diced tomatoes

8 ounces tomato sauce

1 jalapeno, seeded and finely minced

Sour cream, shredded cheddar cheese and additional diced onion for serving

Cook ground beef seasoned with salt and pepper in a large pot over medium–high heat until well browned. Add chili powder, onion, bell pepper, celery, and garlic and cook until vegetables are softened. Stir in kidney beans, diced tomatoes, tomato sauce, and jalapeno; reduce heat to low. Cover and simmer for one hour.

Taste and adjust seasoning as needed. Serve with sour cream, shredded cheese and onion, if desired.

BEEF STEW

Carne Guisada con Vegetales

1 pound beef stew meat or chuck roast cut into 1–inch cubes

½ cup all–purpose flour

2 tablespoons vegetable oil

2 cups beef broth

2 tomatoes, seeded and chopped

2 cloves garlic, minced

8 ounces tomato sauce

1 bay leaf

1 large onion, peeled and chopped

4 large carrots, peeled and cut into 1–inch chunks

2 stalks celery, cut into 1–inch pieces

2 baking potatoes, peeled and cut into 1–inch cubes

1 teaspoon salt

½ teaspoon black pepper

Place the flour in a bowl, add beef and toss to coat well. Add the oil to a large pot over medium heat. Add the beef a few pieces at a time; do not overcrowd. Cook, turning the pieces until beef is browned on all sides, about 5 minutes per batch; add more oil as needed between batches.

Remove the beef from the pot and add the beef broth. Cook over medium–high heat, scraping the pan with a wooden spoon to loosen any browned bits. Add the beef, tomatoes, tomato sauce, garlic, and bay leaves. Bring to a boil, then reduce to a slow simmer.

Cover and cook, skimming broth from time to time, until the beef is tender, about 1 ½ hours. Add the onions, carrots, and celery and simmer, covered for 10 minutes. Add the potatoes and simmer until vegetables are tender, about 30 minutes more. Add broth or water if the stew is dry. Season with salt and pepper to taste.

MEATLOAF
Pastel de Carne

1 medium onion, finely chopped

1 cup finely chopped celery

2 cloves garlic, minced

2 tablespoons vegetable oil

1 ½ pounds lean ground beef

2 slices of white bread, crusts removed and cubed

1 egg, lightly beaten

1 tablespoon Worcestershire sauce

1 tablespoon salt

1 teaspoon black pepper

1 cup frozen peas, thawed

1 cup tomato sauce

Preheat oven to 350° F.

Heat the vegetable oil in a sauté pan over medium heat. Add onions and celery, and cook until softened, about 5 to 7 minutes. Add garlic and cook for an additional minute. Remove from heat and cool slightly.

Place ground beef, bread, egg, Worcestershire sauce, salt, and black pepper in a large bowl. Add cooled vegetables and mix well to combine. Add peas and gently mix together.

Press mixture into an ungreased 8 x 4–inch loaf pan. Spread tomato sauce evenly over the top. Bake for 50 to 60 minutes. Cool for 10 minutes before removing from pan.

Cut into slices and serve.

EASY CHICKEN AND RICE
Arroz con Pollo Facil

1 whole chicken, cut in 8 pieces

2 tablespoons extra virgin olive oil

2 cup prepared jarred salsa

3 cups white rice, rinsed until water runs clear

2 cups chicken broth or water

1 cup frozen peas and carrots, thawed

6 ounce jar pimento-stuffed green olives, drained

2 tablespoons capers, drained

Season chicken liberally with salt and pepper. Heat 2 tablespoons olive oil in a large skillet over medium heat. Add chicken and brown on all sides. Add salsa and chicken stock; stir until warmed. Stir in rice, olives, and capers. Cover pan and cook for 10 to 15 minutes. Add peas and carrots to the top of the rice. Cover and cook for another 5 to 10 minutes until chicken is cooked through and rice is tender. Remove from heat and serve.

SLOW-COOKED SHREDDED BEEF
Ropa Vieja

MEAT INGREDIENTS

1 pound flank steak

1 medium onion, quartered

2 cloves garlic, crushed

1 teaspoon salt

¼ teaspoon black pepper

1 teaspoon dried oregano

3–4 culantro leaves

4 cups beef broth

SAUCE INGREDIENTS

3 tablespoons extra virgin olive oil

2 cloves garlic, minced

1 small onion, thinly sliced

1 green bell pepper, sliced

1 4–ounce jar sliced pimentos, drained

2 culantro leaves

2 tablespoons tomato paste

½ teaspoon achiote seasoning

½ teaspoon dried oregano

Salt and pepper to taste

Add flank steak to a large stock pot with onion, garlic, salt, pepper, oregano, and culantro. Pour beef broth over the top and add more water as needed to cover by 1 inch. Bring to a simmer over medium–high heat. Reduce heat to low, cover and simmer for two hours, or until meat is tender.

Remove meat, reserve broth and discard vegetables. Shred meat into bite–size pieces. Set aside.

Heat oil in a large pan over medium heat. Add garlic and cook for 2 to 3 minutes. Add onion and bell pepper. Sauté for 4 to 5 minutes, or until the vegetables have begun to soften. Stir in pimentos, culantro, tomato paste, achiote, and oregano. Add 1 cup of reserved beef broth and meat to the pan. Stir to combine, then bring to a boil. Reduce heat to low, cover and simmer for 10 minutes. Add more broth as needed, to keep meat mixture moist.

Delicious served with steamed white or yellow rice.

CHICKEN SALAD ROYALE
Ensalada de Pollo Real

4 cups chopped cooked chicken

2 large russet potatoes, boiled, peeled and cubed

16 ounces frozen peas and carrots, thawed and drained

14 ounce can asparagus tips, drained

4 sweet apples, cored and chopped

3 stalks celery, chopped

2 large hard boiled eggs, chopped

3 large hard boiled eggs, sliced

2 cups mayonnaise

½ cup chopped dill pickles

2 tablespoons capers

1 cup pitted green olives

Salt and black pepper to taste

14 ounce can cut beets, drained

1 small head iceberg lettuce

Combine the chicken, potatoes, peas, carrots, asparagus, beets, apples, celery, and chopped eggs in a large mixing bowl. Add the mayonnaise, pickles, capers, and olives and stir well to combine. Add more mayonnaise as needed. Season to taste with salt and black pepper. Refrigerate for 2 to 3 hours.

For serving, prepare a large platter with iceberg lettuce leaves. Sprinkle drained beets over the lettuce leaves. Spoon the prepared chicken salad over the top and decorate with sliced eggs.

CHICKEN A LA KING
Pollo al Rey

4 tablespoons butter

2 egg yolks

4 ounces mushrooms, sliced

2 cups cooked chicken, cubed

1 bell pepper, thinly sliced

4 ounce jar sliced pimentos, drained

1 clove garlic, minced

½ cup frozen peas, thawed

¼ cup all–purpose flour

½ cup pimento stuffed olives, drained and chopped

1 cup whole milk

2 sheets frozen puff pastry dough, thawed

1 cup chicken broth

1 egg, beaten with 2 tablespoons water

1 teaspoon salt

½ teaspoon black pepper

Melt butter in a large saucepan over medium heat. Add mushrooms and sauté until browned. Add green peppers and garlic; cook for another 5 to 6 minutes until softened. Add flour and cook for 4 to 5 minutes, stirring constantly. Slowly whisk in milk and chicken broth, avoiding lumps. Season with salt and pepper. Bring the mixture to a boil and cook for 1 to 2 minutes or until the mixture has thickened. Remove from heat and quickly whisk in egg yolks until well combined.

Return to the heat, add cooked chicken, pimentos, peas, and olives. Bring to a simmer, reduce heat to low and cook for 5 minutes. Adjust seasoning as needed. Keep warm and prepare shells.

Preheat oven to 425° F. Beat egg and water together in a small bowl.

Cut six squares, approximately 5" x 5", from each sheet of puff pastry using a sharp knife. Place each square on an ungreased baking sheet. Using a sharp paring knife, lightly score a 1–inch border around each square. Brush each square with egg mixture.

Bake in the preheated oven until puffed and golden, 20 to 25 minutes. Carefully remove the center of each pastry and save for garnish, if desired. Spoon in prepared filling into each shell and serve.

The filling is also delicious served over rice, noodles, toast or as a filling for a pot pie.

ROAST CHICKEN
Pollo Relleno

CHICKEN

1 whole chicken, 3 – 3 ½ pounds

1 tablespoon Worcestershire sauce

1 tablespoon white vinegar

2 cloves garlic, minced

¼ cup olive oil

½ teaspoon salt

¼ teaspoon black pepper

3 carrots, peeled and cut into 2–inch pieces

1 medium onion, quartered

2 large russet potatoes, peeled and cut into 2–inch pieces

STUFFING

½ pound ground pork

¼ pound cooked ham, finely chopped

1 green bell pepper, seeded and chopped

1 tablespoon capers, drained

1 tablespoon chopped dill pickles

2 tablespoons dark raisins

½ teaspoon salt

¼ teaspoon black pepper

1 cup dry white wine

Preheat oven to 350° F.

Wash chicken inside and out and pat dry with a paper towel.

Add Worcestershire sauce, vinegar, olive oil, salt, pepper, and garlic to a small bowl and stir to combine. Rub mixture all over the chicken. Set aside to marinate.

Combine pork, ham, bell pepper, capers, pickles, raisins, salt, and pepper together in a bowl. Stuff the cavity of the chicken with the mixture. Place chicken in a roasting pan. Scatter potatoes, carrots, and onion around the chicken. Pour white wine around the chicken.

Bake for 60 to 75 minutes, or until the stuffing is cooked through. Remove from the oven, cover loosely with aluminum foil and rest for 15 minutes. Remove the stuffing, carve the chicken and serve with the roasted vegetables.

Prepare a pan sauce, if desired.

CHRISTMAS TURKEY
Pavo de Navidad

20 to 22 pound turkey, cleaned and dried

5 green onions, thinly sliced

2 cups dry white wine

4 stalks celery, chopped

2 pounds loin of pork, trimmed of excess fat

28 ounce can diced tomatoes, drained

2 pound eye of round

2 6–ounce cans tomato paste

Turkey neck and giblets, except liver

1 cup dark raisins

5 cloves of garlic

1 cup blanched almonds

1 large onion

16 ounces stuffed green olives, drained

1 tablespoon salt

4 ounces capers, drained

4 slices bacon

¼ cup achiote oil

2 large green bell peppers, seeded and chopped

Salt and ground black pepper

If desired, inject turkey with white wine and allow to marinate for 24 hours before roasting.

Place the pork, beef, and turkey neck and giblets in a large stock pot with the salt, garlic, and onion. Cover with cold water. Bring to a boil over high heat, reduce heat to low and simmer one hour or until meat is tender. Drain, discard garlic and onion, reserving 2 cups of cooking liquid. Cool slightly.

Cut or shred meat into large chunks, add to the bowl of a food processor fitted with a steel blade. Process meat in batches until the meat has the texture of cooked ground beef. Add a small amount of cooking liquid as needed to help process the meat. Transfer to a large mixing bowl.

Cook bacon in a large skillet until crisp. Remove bacon from pan and set aside to drain. Add the green peppers, scallions, and celery to the pan with the bacon fat, cook for 5 to 6 minutes until vegetables are slightly softened. Set aside to cool.

Add cooled vegetables to the meat mixture along with tomatoes, tomato paste, raisins, almonds, olives, capers, pimento, and reserved bacon. Mix very well to combine.

Place the turkey breast side up on a rack in a large roasting pan. Stuff turkey cavities with prepared meat mixture. Place any excess stuffing around the turkey in the roasting pan. Brush the turkey with achiote oil and season the outside of the turkey with salt and pepper. Add one cup of water or white wine to the pan.

Bake at 325° F, until a meat thermometer registers 170° F in the breast or stuffing and 180° F in the thigh, about 5 hours. When the turkey is about ⅔ done, loosely cover the breast with a piece of foil to prevent overcooking. Lift turkey onto platter and let stand for 15 minutes before carving.
Remove stuffing from the turkey and serve with sliced turkey.

SPAGHETTI WITH SPICY MEAT SAUCE

Spaghetti con Salsa de Carne Picante

¼ pound sliced bacon, cut in 1–inch pieces

1 pound lean ground beef

1 green pepper, chopped

2 medium onions, minced

1 jalapeno pepper, seeded and minced

1 clove garlic, minced

1 tablespoon chili powder

1 small can sliced mushrooms, drained

8 ounce can tomato sauce

6 ounce can tomato paste

1 cup water

1 pound dried spaghetti

½ cup grated Parmesan cheese

Salt and pepper to taste

Cook chopped bacon in a large skillet over medium heat until browned and lightly crisped. Add ground beef and season with salt and pepper; cook until browned, about 7 to 10 minutes. Add onion, green pepper, jalapeno, and garlic, cooking until onion and peppers have softened. Season with chili powder, salt and pepper and cook for 1 to 2 minutes. Add mushrooms, tomato sauce, tomato paste, and water. Reduce heat to low and simmer uncovered for 15 minutes, or until sauce has thickened.

While meat mixture simmers, cook spaghetti in a large stock pot of boiling salted water. Cook according to package directions until al dente. Drain pasta and mix together with meat mixture in a large bowl.

Sprinkle with grated cheese and serve.

SPAGHETTI WITH CREAMY CHEESE SAUCE

Macarrones con Salsa de Queso

12 ounces uncooked spaghetti

4 tablespoons butter

1 tablespoon cornstarch

1 cup whole milk

¼ pound cheddar cheese, shredded

¼ teaspoon black pepper

2 large egg yolks

¼ cup grated Parmesan cheese

Salt and black pepper to taste

Preheat oven to 350° F. Coat a baking dish with butter or cooking spray. Set aside.

Cook spaghetti in boiling salted water until al dente, about 10 to 12 minutes.

While pasta cooks, melt butter in a sauce pan over medium heat. Whisk in cornstarch. Slowly whisk in the milk to avoid clumps. Bring the mixture to a low simmer, add the cheddar cheese and black pepper and stir until cheese has melted and a smooth sauce has formed. Remove from heat and cool slightly. Quickly stir in egg yolks to avoid scrambling the eggs. Cover and keep warm until the pasta is finished cooking.

Drain the pasta well. Add back to the pot and stir in the prepared cheese sauce. Pour the mixture into the prepared baking dish and sprinkle with grated Parmesan cheese. Bake for 15 to 20 minutes, or until bubbling around the edges and a light brown crust has formed.

MACARONI MILANESE
Macarrones a la Milanesa

1 pound elbow macaroni

6 ounces tomato paste

2 tablespoons butter

1 tablespoon chopped capers

8 ounces mushrooms, sliced

¼ cup chopped green olives

2 medium onions, chopped

1 tablespoon white vinegar

2 large green bell peppers, chopped

1 tablespoon Worcestershire sauce

4 stalks celery, minced

½ cup grated Parmesan cheese

2 carrots, grated

Salt and ground black pepper

3 cloves garlic, minced

1 pound lean ground beef

1 cup dry red wine

Heat two tablespoons of butter in a deep skillet over medium high heat. Add sliced mushrooms and cook until browned. Add onions, celery, bell peppers, and carrots to the pan, season with salt and pepper and cook until vegetables have softened. Add garlic and cook until fragrant, about 1 minute. Remove vegetables from the pan.

Add the ground beef to the pan, season with salt and pepper. Cook for 8 to 10 minutes, until ground beef is browned. Add red wine to the pan and allow to reduce by half. Add tomato paste, stir to combine and cook for 3 to 4 minutes. Stir in reserved vegetables along with the capers, olives, vinegar, and Worcestershire sauce. Cover and reduce heat and simmer while macaroni cooks.

Prepare elbow macaroni according to package instructions. Drain completely. Add macaroni to the meat sauce and stir to combine.

Sprinkle with Parmesan cheese and serve.

SAVORY STUFFED CANNELLONI
Canelones Rellenos

1 pound of cannelloni pasta

1 pound of ground pork

1 pound of ground beef

2 medium onions, diced

2 green peppers, diced

4 cloves garlic, minced

1 6-ounce can tomato paste

16 ounces prepared marinara sauce

1 cup water

1 egg, beaten

1 cup grated Parmesan cheese, divided

Salt and black pepper

In a large skillet, sauté the ground pork and ground beef until browned, breaking up large pieces of meat. Season with salt and pepper. Add onions, peppers, and garlic and cook until vegetables have softened. Stir in tomato paste, marinara sauce, and water. Cook for 10 to 15 minutes until mixture has thickened slightly. Quickly stir in beaten egg and 3 tablespoons of Parmesan cheese. Remove from heat and cool.

Preheat oven to 350° F. Grease a 13 x 9-inch baking dish.

Stuff each cannelloni with the cooled meat mixture and place into the baking dish. Top the cannelloni with the remaining meat mixture and sprinkle with remaining Parmesan cheese. Cover with aluminum foil and bake for 20 minutes. Remove foil and bake for another 10 minutes until golden brown.

DESSERTS

EASY RUM CAKE
Dulce de Ron Facil

CAKE

1 cup finely chopped walnuts or pecans

1 box yellow cake mix

4 large eggs

½ cup water

½ cup vegetable oil

¾ cup Panamanian dark rum

GLAZE

1 cup granulated sugar

½ cup butter

½ cup Panamanian dark rum

¼ cup water

Preheat oven to 325° F. Grease a Bundt pan with butter or non-stick cooking spray.

Pour the chopped nuts evenly into the bottom of the pan.

Mix together cake mix, eggs, water, oil, and rum in a mixing bowl. Beat for 2 minutes with an electric mixer. Pour prepared batter into the pan. Bake for 50 to 60 minutes, until a cake tester inserted into the center of the cake comes out clean. Remove from oven and allow to cool for 5 minutes.

Prepare glaze while cake cools. Combine all glaze ingredients in a medium saucepan and bring to a boil over medium heat. Reduce heat and stir until sugar is dissolved. Pour hot glaze evenly over cake.

Cool cake completely before inverting cake onto a serving platter. Dust cake with powdered sugar, if desired.

VINEGAR SUGAR COOKIES
Galletas de Vinagre

1 cup butter, softened

¾ cup granulated sugar

1 large egg

1 teaspoon vanilla extract

1 tablespoon white vinegar

2 cups all-purpose flour

½ teaspoon ground nutmeg

1 teaspoon baking soda

Colored sugar or sprinkles (optional)

Preheat oven to 350° F. Line two baking sheets with parchment paper.

In the bowl of a mixer, beat the butter and sugar together until creamy. Beat in the egg, vanilla, and vinegar. Gradually add the flour, nutmeg, and baking soda and beat on medium speed until combined.

Roll into 1-inch balls and place 2 inches apart onto the prepared baking sheet. Flatten each ball to about ¼-inch thickness. Repeat with remaining dough. Bake 8 to 10 minutes, until cookies are set and edges are golden. Cool for one minute, then remove to a wire rack to cool completely.

Store cookies in an airtight container.

MERINGUE COOKIES
Merengues

3 large egg whites, room temperature

1 teaspoon vanilla extract

¼ teaspoon cream of tartar

Pinch of salt

⅔ cup granulated sugar

Preheat oven to 200° F. Line two baking sheets with parchment paper.

Add the egg whites, vanilla, salt, and cream of tartar to a large mixing bowl. Beat until the mixture is frothy and soft peaks form. Gradually add the sugar 1 tablespoon at a time, beating for 15 seconds between each addition. Once all of the sugar has been added, beat for an additional 5 to 7 minutes, until stiff and glossy.

Transfer the mixture to a large pastry bag fitted with a star tip. Pipe 1 ½–inch cookies onto the lined baking sheets, leaving 1 inch between each cookie.

Bake for 45 minutes until firm. Turn off oven, leaving meringues in the oven for 1 hour.

Remove and cool completely before storing in an airtight container.

COCONUT CANDY
Cocadas Panameñas

1 cup honey

2 cups grated unsweetened coconut

2 cinnamon sticks

Spray a baking sheet with non–stick cooking spray. Set aside.

Mix honey and coconut together in a saucepan. Add cinnamon sticks. Bring mixture to a boil over medium heat. Continue stirring until honey begins to caramelize and mixture turns a deep golden color, about 5 minutes.

Pour the mixture on to the prepared baking sheet and remove cinnamon sticks. Cool to room temperature.

Coat your hands with cooking spray. Roll rounded tablespoons of the mixture into small balls, placing each ball into a paper liner. Serve at room temperature.

MELT AWAY COOKIES
Galletas Que Se Disuelven En La Boca

1 pound cornstarch

1 cup granulated sugar

1 teaspoon ground cinnamon

3 large eggs, lightly beaten

¼ cup butter, melted and cooled

½ teaspoon vanilla extract

Preheat oven to 350° F. Line two baking sheets with parchment paper.

Sift the cornstarch, granulated sugar, and cinnamon together into a large mixing bowl. Add the eggs, vanilla, and butter and stir together until it forms a stiff dough. Break off pieces of dough and roll into a thin 3–inch rope. Shape each rope into a spiral and place on the prepared baking sheet.

Bake for 15 to 20 minutes, or until lightly golden. Remove to a rack to cool completely.

Store in an airtight container.

PECAN SANDIES
Sandies de Nueces

1 cup butter, softened

⅓ cup granulated sugar

¼ teaspoon salt

2 teaspoons water

2 teaspoons vanilla extract

2 cups all–purpose flour

2 cups ground pecans

2 cups powdered sugar, sifted

In a large mixing bowl, beat butter and granulated sugar together until creamy. Add salt, water, vanilla, flour, and pecans and mix well. Cover and chill dough for one hour.

Preheat oven to 325° F. Line two baking sheets with parchment paper.

Form chilled dough into small balls, about 1–inch in diameter. Place on a baking sheet 1–inch apart. Bake for 12 to 14 minutes. Allow cookies to cool slightly then roll in powdered sugar.

Cool completely and store in an airtight container.

PINEAPPLE CAKE

Dulce de Piña

1 cup butter, softened

2 cups granulated sugar

4 large eggs, separated

1 ½ cups crushed pineapple in juice, drained well

1 teaspoon vanilla extract

½ teaspoon lemon extract

¼ teaspoon almond extract

3 ½ cups all-purpose flour

½ teaspoon baking soda

1 tablespoon baking powder

½ teaspoon salt

Preheat oven to 350° F. Coat a 13 x 9–inch pan with non–stick cooking spray.

In a medium mixing bowl, beat egg whites to stiff peaks, being careful not to over beat. Set aside.

Whisk together flour, baking soda, baking powder, and salt in a small bowl. In another large bowl, beat butter and sugar together until mixture is creamy. Add egg yolks one at a time, beating after each addition. Add crushed pineapple and extracts and mix well. Beat in flour mixture, just until combined. Fold in reserved egg whites until well incorporated, preserving as much volume as possible.

Pour batter into the prepared pan. Bake for 25 to 30 minutes or until a cake tester inserted into the center of the cake comes out clean.

Cool completely on a wire rack.

TRES LECHES CAKE
Dulce de Tres Leches

1 cup all-purpose flour

1 ½ teaspoons baking powder

¼ teaspoon salt

5 large eggs, room temperature

1 cup granulated sugar, divided

1 teaspoon vanilla extract

⅓ cup whole milk

1 can evaporated milk

1 can sweetened condensed milk

2 cups heavy cream

¼ cup powdered sugar

Strawberries, raspberries or maraschino cherries for garnish

Preheat oven to 350° F. Coat a 13 x 9-inch glass baking dish with non-stick cooking spray. Set aside.

Add flour, baking powder, and salt to a large bowl. Whisk to combine. Separate eggs into two mixing bowls. Beat egg whites on high speed until soft peaks form. Slowly add ¼ cup sugar and beat until egg whites form stiff peaks, but are not dry.

Beat egg yolks with remaining ¾ cup sugar on high speed until yolks are pale yellow. Stir in milk and vanilla extract. Pour egg yolk mixture over the flour mixture and stir gently to combine. Fold in egg whites just until combined. Spread mixture evenly in the prepared pan.

Bake for 25 to 30 minutes or until a cake tester inserted into the center comes out clean. Cool cake on a rack for 5 minutes then gently pierce the cake all over with a skewer or fork.

Combine evaporated milk, condensed milk, and ¼ cup heavy cream in a small pitcher. Slowly drizzle the milk mixture over the top and sides of the cake.

Cover and place cake in the refrigerator and allow the cake to absorb the milk mixture for 2 hours or overnight.

To ice the cake, whip the remaining 1 ¾ cup heavy cream with powdered sugar until thick and spreadable. Spread over the surface of the cake. Decorate cake with fruit, if desired. Cut into squares and serve.

EASY PINEAPPLE UPSIDE-DOWN CAKE

Bolteado de Piña Facil

¼ cup butter

1 cup packed brown sugar

1 20–ounce can crushed pineapple in juice, drained, juice reserved

1 6–ounce jar maraschino cherries, without stems

1 box yellow cake mix

3 eggs

½ cup vegetable oil

Preheat oven to 350° F.

In 13 x 9–inch pan, melt butter in oven. Sprinkle brown sugar evenly over butter. Arrange cherries evenly over the brown sugar. Sprinkle crushed pineapple evenly over brown sugar.

Add enough water to reserved pineapple juice to measure 1 cup, if needed. In a mixing bowl, combine the cake mix, eggs, vegetable oil, and pineapple juice. Mix well to combine. Pour batter over the pineapple and cherries, spreading evenly.

Bake for 40 to 45 minutes or until a cake tester inserted into the center of the cake comes out clean. Immediately run knife around side of pan to loosen cake. Place heatproof serving plate upside down onto pan; turn plate and pan over. Leave pan over cake for 5 minutes so brown sugar and pineapple topping can drizzle over cake; remove pan. Cool 30 minutes.

Serve warm or cool. Store covered in refrigerator.

ANGEL FOOD CAKE WITH STRAWBERRY GLAZE

Angel Food Cake con Glaseado de Fresas

CAKE

1 ¼ cups egg whites (about 8 or 9 eggs)

¼ teaspoon salt

1 teaspoon cream of tartar

1 ½ cups granulated sugar

1 cup cake flour, sifted

1 teaspoon almond extract

½ teaspoon almond extract

STRAWBERRY SAUCE

1 pint fresh strawberries

3 tablespoons sugar

1 tablespoon corn starch

¼ cup water

1 tablespoon lemon juice

Preheat oven to 350° F. Place oven rack in lowest position.

Sift together flour and ½ cup sugar. Repeat several times. Set aside.

Place room temperature egg whites in a large bowl. Add cream of tartar, extracts, and salt to egg whites; beat on medium speed until soft peaks form. Gradually add 1 cup sugar, about 2 tablespoons at a time, beating on high until stiff peaks form. Gradually fold in flour mixture, about 1/2 cup at a time.

Gently spoon into an ungreased 10-inch tube pan. Cut through batter with a knife to remove air pockets. Bake until lightly browned and entire top appears dry, 35–40 minutes. Immediately invert pan; cool completely, about 1 hour. Prepare strawberry sauce while cake cools.

Mash strawberries; set aside. Combine the sugar, cornstarch, and water in a small saucepan until smooth. Bring to a boil over medium heat; cook and stir for 2 minutes or until thickened. Stir in strawberries; remove from the heat. Stir in lemon juice. Transfer to a small bowl. Refrigerate until chilled.

When cake has cooled, run a knife around side and center tube of pan. Remove cake to a serving plate. Cut into slices and serve with cooled strawberry sauce.

STRAWBERRY CHEESECAKE
Cheesecake de Fresas

1 7–ounce package Maria cookies

¼ cup melted butter

6 large eggs, separated

2 cups granulated sugar

1 cup small curd cottage cheese

8 ounces cream cheese, room temperature

1 cup sour cream

1 tablespoon vanilla extract

21–ounce can strawberry pie filling,
or other favorite flavor

Preheat oven to 350° F.

Place Maria cookies in the bowl of a food processor and process until fine crumbs form. Add melted butter and pulse until the mixture is the consistency of wet sand. Transfer mixture to a 13 x 9–inch glass baking pan and press crumbs firmly onto the bottom of the pan.

In a large bowl, beat egg whites until stiff peaks form. Set aside.

Add the cottage cheese to a bowl of a food processor fitted with a steel blade. Process cottage cheese until smooth. Transfer to a large mixing bowl and add the sugar, cream cheese, sour cream, and vanilla and beat until well combined. Carefully fold in the egg whites, preserving as much of the volume as possible. Pour the mixture over the prepared crust and spread evenly. Bake for one hour until just set in the center. Remove from oven to a cooling rack and allow to cool completely.

Refrigerate for four hours or more. Remove from refrigerator and top with strawberry topping. Cut into squares and serve.

CARROT CAKE
Pastel de Zanahorias

1 ½ cups all–purpose flour

2 tablespoons baking soda

2 tablespoons ground cinnamon

1 teaspoon salt

2 cups granulated sugar

1 ½ cups vegetable oil

2 tablespoons vanilla extract

4 large eggs

3 cups finely grated carrots

½ cup chopped walnuts

1 ½ cup mincemeat

Preheat oven to 350° F. Grease a 9–inch square or round baking pan with cooking spray. Line the bottom of the pan with parchment paper.

Sift together flour, baking soda, cinnamon, and salt in a large mixing bowl. In another bowl, combine the sugar, vegetable oil, vanilla, and eggs using an electric mixer on medium speed just until combined. With the mixer on low speed, add the flour mixture and incorporate well. Fold in the carrots, walnuts, and mince-meat just until combined.

Pour the mixture into the prepared pan and bake for 40 to 45 minutes, until a skewer inserted in the center comes out clean. Remove from oven and cool completely. Frost cooled cake with cream cheese frosting, if desired.

OLD-FASHIONED APPLE PIE

Pie de Manzana Tradicional

FILLING

4 to 5 large tart apples, peeled and cored

½ cup granulated sugar

1 teaspoon ground cinnamon

¼ teaspoon ground nutmeg

½ teaspoon salt

2 tablespoons all–purpose flour

1 tablespoon lemon juice

1 tablespoon butter

PIE CRUST

2 ¼ cup all–purpose flour, sifted

¾ cup vegetable shortening

1 teaspoon salt

¼ cup ice water

1 large egg, beaten

1 tablespoon granulated sugar

Measure the vegetable shortening and place it in the refrigerator while you prepare the flour mixture. Place the flour and salt in the bowl of a food processor fitted with a steel blade and pulse a few times to mix. Add the shortening. Pulse 8 to 12 times, until the mixture is the size of peas. With the machine running, pour the ice water down the feed tube and pulse the machine until the dough begins to form a ball. Pour mixture out on a floured board and roll into a ball. Wrap in plastic wrap and refrigerate for 30 minutes.

Cut the dough in half. Roll each piece on a well–floured board into a circle, rolling from the center to the edge, turning and flouring the dough to make sure it doesn't stick to the board. Fold the dough in half, place in a 9–inch pie pan, unfold to fit the pan. Repeat with the top crust and refrigerate both and prepare the filling.

In a small bowl, combine the sugar, flour, and spices; set aside.

Cut apples in half and slice into ¼-inch slices. Add to a large bowl and toss with lemon juice. Pour sugar mixture over the apples, toss to coat.

Fill the prepared crust with apple mixture and dot with butter. Cover with top crust. Trim, seal and crimp edges as desired. Cut several steam vent holes in crust. Brush with beaten egg, and sprinkle with sugar.

Bake in an oven preheated to 375° F until crust is brown and juices are bubbling, about 1 hour. Let cool on wire rack before serving.

PUMPKIN CUSTARD
Natillas de Calabaza

15 ounce can pumpkin puree

2 tablespoons melted butter

1 cup heavy cream

1 cup granulated sugar

1 cup all-purpose flour

4 eggs, lightly beaten

¼ teaspoon salt

2 teaspoons vanilla extract

Preheat oven to 350° F. Butter an 8-inch round cake pan.

Combine all ingredients in a medium bowl and mix thoroughly. Pour the mixture into the prepared mold. Bake for 40 to 45 minutes, or until the center is set and a knife inserted into the center comes out clean.

Cool completely on a wire rack then invert onto a cake plate for serving.

FRUIT COCKTAIL CUSTARD
Flan de Cóctel de Frutas

6 large eggs

1 ½ cups granulated sugar, divided

1 cup whole milk

½ teaspoon salt

2 teaspoons vanilla extract

¼ teaspoon ground nutmeg

1 20-ounce can fruit cocktail in syrup, drained

Preheat oven to 350° F.

Beat eggs in a large bowl. Add 1 cup sugar, milk, salt, vanilla, nutmeg, and drained fruit cocktail. Mix well to combine. Set aside.

Add remaining ½ cup of sugar and reserved syrup to a small saucepan. Bring mixture to a boil and allow sugar to caramelize. Carefully pour hot syrup into a 9-inch round glass baking dish, turning the dish to evenly coat the bottom and sides.

Place the dish in a larger baking pan. Pour boiling water into larger pan to a depth of 1 inch. Bake for 45 to 50 minutes or until center is just set.

Remove dish from a larger pan to a wire rack; cool for 1 hour. Cover and refrigerate at least 8 hours.

To unmold, run a knife around edges and invert onto a large rimmed serving platter. Cut into wedges or spoon onto dessert plates; spoon sauce over each serving.

LEMON MERINGUE PIE
Pie de Limón con Merengue

PIE CRUST

1 cup all-purpose flour

½ teaspoon salt

⅓ cup vegetable shortening

3 to 4 tablespoons ice water

FILLING

⅓ cup all-purpose flour

⅓ cup cornstarch

1 ½ cups granulated sugar

1 ½ cups water

3 large egg yolks

½ cup fresh lemon juice

1 tablespoon lemon zest

3 tablespoons butter

MERINGUE TOPPING

3 large egg whites, room temperature

¼ teaspoon cream of tartar

6 tablespoons granulated sugar

½ teaspoon vanilla extract

Prepare the crust. Place the flour and salt in the bowl of a food processor fitted with a steel blade and pulse a few times to mix. Add the shortening. Pulse 8 to 12 times, until the mixture is the size of peas. With the machine running, pour the ice water down the feed tube and pulse the machine until the dough begins to form a ball. Pour mixture out on a floured board and roll into a ball. Wrap in plastic wrap and refrigerate for 30 minutes.

Heat oven to 450° F.

Roll pastry on lightly floured surface into a round 2 inches larger than upside-down 9-inch glass pie plate. Fold pastry in half and transfer to pie plate. Unfold pastry and ease into plate, pressing firmly against bottom and side. Trim overhanging edge of pastry leaving 1 extra inch from rim of pie plate. Fold excess pastry under and crimp as desired. Prick bottom and side of pastry thoroughly with fork. Bake 13 to 15 minutes or until light brown; cool on cooling rack.

Reduce oven temperature to 350° F.

Prepare the filling. Beat egg yolks in a small bowl. In medium saucepan, mix sugar, flour and the cornstarch; gradually stir in water. Cook over medium heat, stirring constantly, until mixture thickens and boils. Boil and stir 1 minute. Immediately stir with whisk at least half of hot mixture into egg yolks; stir back into hot mixture in saucepan. Return to boiling; boil and stir constantly for 2 minutes; remove from heat. Stir in butter, lemon zest and lemon juice with whisk. Cover and keep warm and prepare the meringue.

In medium bowl, beat egg whites and cream of tartar with electric mixer on high speed until foamy. Add sugar, 1 tablespoon at a time, occasionally scraping the side of the bowl. Continue beating until stiff, glossy peaks form and sugar is completely dissolved. Beat in vanilla extract. Pour the hot filling into baked pie shell. Immediately spread meringue onto hot filling to cover top completely, spreading to edge of crust to seal the filling and prevent shrinkage.

Bake 20 to 25 minutes or until meringue is lightly browned. Cool on cooling rack 1 hour. Refrigerate about 4 hours or until filling is set. Store loosely covered in refrigerator.

HOMESTYLE VANILLA FLAN
Flan Casero de Vainilla

1 cup granulated sugar

10 large eggs

3 12–ounce cans evaporated milk

2 14–ounce cans sweetened condensed milk

2 teaspoons vanilla extract

Preheat oven to 350° F.

Pour sugar into a small saucepan over medium heat. Slowly cook the sugar, carefully swirling the pan occasionally until evenly caramelized. Pour the caramel into a 13 x 9–inch glass baking dish. Quickly swirl the baking dish to evenly distribute the caramel. Set aside.

In a large bowl, lightly whisk together eggs, milks, and vanilla, incorporating as little air as possible to avoid bubbles. Pour mixture over the prepared caramel.

Place the baking dish inside a larger roasting pan. Carefully pour 4 to 6 cups of very hot water into the roasting pan, creating a water bath. Bake for 25 to 30 minutes, or until the flan is barely set in the middle.

Cool completely and refrigerate for a minimum of 4 hours before serving.

COCONUT CUSTARD
Flan de Coco

1 14-ounce can coconut milk

4 large eggs

2 large egg yolks

2 ¾ cups granulated sugar, divided

1 cup water

1 teaspoon vanilla extract

In a large heavy saucepan, cook and stir ¾ cup sugar over low heat until sugar is melted and golden. Pour the caramel into a 9-inch glass pie plate or 6 individual custard cups, quickly rotating the pie plate or cups to cover the bottom with caramel.

Combine coconut milk, eggs, egg yolks, 2 cups sugar, water, and vanilla extract together in a mixing bowl until well blended. Pour mixture over caramel.

Place the dish in a larger baking pan. Pour boiling water into larger pan to a depth of 1 inch. Bake at 350° F for 40 to 45 minutes or until center is just set.

Remove dish from a larger pan to a wire rack; cool for 1 hour. Cover and refrigerate at least 8 hours.

To unmold, run a knife around edges and invert onto a large rimmed serving platter. Cut into wedges or spoon onto dessert plates; spoon caramel sauce over each serving.

BREAD PUDDING
Pudín de Pan

3 cups of cubed baguette, crusts removed and cut into 1–inch pieces

2 large eggs, lightly beaten

12 ounces evaporated milk

14 ounces sweetened condensed milk

2 tablespoons vanilla extract

2 tablespoons melted butter

1 teaspoon ground cinnamon

⅛ teaspoon ground nutmeg

15–ounce can fruit cocktail, drained and liquid reserved

½ cup dark raisins

1 cup granulated sugar

Preheat oven to 350° F. Brush the inside of a casserole dish with butter.

Mix together the eggs, evaporated milk, sweetened condensed milk, vanilla, cinnamon, nutmeg, and melted butter in a pitcher. Place bread cubes into a large mixing bowl. Pour milk mixture over the bread and stir to combine. Let the bread soak for 15 minutes. Stir in fruit cocktail and raisins. Pour mixture into the baking dish and bake for 1 hour, or until the center is set. Cover with aluminum foil, if needed, to prevent over browning.

While the bread pudding bakes, combine the reserved juice from the fruit cocktail with the 1 cup of sugar together in a medium saucepan. Bring to a boil, reduce heat and simmer for 10 minutes until thickened.

Remove bread pudding from the oven and cool for 15 minutes. Drizzle sauce over the top of the bread pudding and serve warm.